GRAND CANYON WILDFLOWERS

by Arthur M. Phillips, III

photography by John Richardson
Southern Illinois University

Edited and coordinated by Timothy J. Priehs
Book design by Christina Watkins
Printed by Lorraine Press, Inc.

Cover photograph by Jack W. Dykinga

Inset photograph—Common sunflower
by John Richardson

Spruce-fir photograph, page 1, and
Inner Canyon photograph, page 2,
by Arthur Phillips

Ponderosa photograph, page 1,
by Robert Butterfield

All other photography by John Richardson

Revised edition 1990

*This book is dedicated to
the late Walter B. McDougall, former
National Park Service naturalist and
ecologist and curator of botany at the
Museum of Northern Arizona. Named
Eminent Ecologist of 1977 by the
Ecological Society of America, his love
affair with plants spanned seven
decades. Author of the first popular
guide to the wildflowers of Grand
Canyon National Park and expert on
the flora of northern Arizona, Dr.
McDougall served as an inspiration to
all who were privileged to know and
work with him.*

PREFACE

The problem with wildflower books that cover anything more than a few acres of flat ground is that they are either overwhelming or incomplete. We make no pretense of solving the dilemma. However, we hope that this book will increase your enjoyment of the Grand Canyon and perhaps add a dimension to your visit that many people overlook.

We have endeavored to serve two purposes: first, to help you identify some of the common wildflowers that you are likely to encounter, whether you visit the South Rim, the North Rim, hike the Inner Canyon trails, or run the river; and second, the book is a pictorial essay exploring the beauty and diversity of the flowering plants found in the park. Some of the plants will be seen by virtually every visitor. Others are so rare or are found in such limited, inaccessible areas that few people ever see them, and photographs of them have never before been published in a popular guide.

The book is organized by flower color. Within each color the plants are arranged in the order used in most botanical manuals. This arrangement makes it easy to quickly thumb through a particular color to identify a flower, and it places closely related species together within each section.

A word about terminology: every effort has been made to avoid scientific terms in the descriptions. Readers who wish a more technical description are urged to consult *Arizona Flora* by Kearney and Peebles, *Seed Plants of Northern Arizona* by McDougall, or *The Cacti of Arizona* by Benson. The first two are not illustrated; Benson provides photographs of many of the cacti.

The scientific names used follow *Annotated Checklist of Vascular Plants of Grand Canyon National Park 1987* by Phillips, Phillips, and Bernzott. Common names are variable and are not standardized; they have come from a combination of sources listed in the bibliography.

Many people deserve thanks for their help and support in the preparation of this book. Dr. Barbara Phillips participated in every phase, from the inception of the field work to editing the manuscript. Timothy J. Priehs provided support and encouragement throughout the project. Donald Kurz, Jill Downs, Elaine Peterson, and George and Karen Zins have all helped in one way or another. The National Park Service has cooperated fully in the preparation of this book. Finally, Dr. Walter B. McDougall provided inspiration and invaluable help in all stages of the work.

Arthur M. Phillips, III
Flagstaff, Arizona
November 1978; October 1989

I wish to express my appreciation to Dr. Michael Dingerson of Southern Illinois University and Tim Priehs of the Grand Canyon Natural History Association for giving me their cooperation and the opportunity to do the photography for this book.

I am indebted to Karen Schmitt for taking over my duties of the facility while I was at the Grand Canyon, and to Heather R. Barrett for cataloging the slides and keeping them all in order.

I would like to thank the following personnel from the Grand Canyon National Park: Trinkle Jones, Robert Euler and Dave Ochsner for not only their help but their friendship.

My thanks and appreciation to Art and Barbara Phillips for the double pleasure of the many hikes and of working with them on this book.

John Richardson
Director of Research
Photography and Illustration
Facility and Associate Professor
of Botany
Southern Illinois University
Carbondale, Illinois

Leave Them For Those Who Follow

An important word of caution: picking wildflowers, digging up plants, or otherwise disturbing natural objects in a national park is strictly prohibited. Look at them, photograph them, enjoy them as they are, and leave them to give similar pleasure to those who follow you. Just as important, leave them to play their natural role of providing pollen for bees, food for hungry birds in winter, and seeds from which next year's flowers will come.

The information given in this book on Native American and pioneer uses of plants is intended only as a matter of interest. Similarly, grazing of domestic livestock is not permitted in the park, and notes on the palatability of certain plants pertain to their use by livestock outside the national park.

CONTENTS

INTRODUCTION

Grand Canyon National Park contains over 1400 different kinds of plants, a diversity directly attributable to the great variety of its natural habitats. Within an elevational difference of almost 8000 feet, plant communities vary from subalpine in the cool, moist forests and meadows of the North Rim to Mohave Desert in the hot, dry Inner Gorge. Such contrasts are rarely found within as short a horizontal distance as they are here.

The reason, of course, for the contrast in vegetation is the difference in climate caused by the contrast in elevation. The high Kaibab Plateau on the North Rim gathers deep snow during the long winter, and receives frequent rain from thunderstorms occurring almost daily in July and August. Nearly 30 inches of rain per year fall on the North Rim. The South Rim, 1000 feet or so lower, measures about half as much annual rainfall, and the snows of winter

are usually short-lived. The warmer-drier pattern continues as elevations decrease within the Canyon reaching extremes in the Inner Gorge, where the rims cause a rainshadow and the walls of black schist heat the Canyon like an oven. Very few species of plants occur both on the rims and along the river: the desert plants cannot survive the snow and frigid winter temperatures of the rims, and the forest species cannot survive the scorching dry heat of summer in the Inner Gorge.

NORTH RIM

Punctuated by mountain meadows in shallow valleys, stately forests of Engelmann spruce and subalpine fir prevail on the North Rim above elevations of 8500 feet. The deep snows of winter linger late in the dense, shady forests; while the meadows, when the warm spring sun dries them out, take on hues of green, yellow, and blue as the colorful procession of spring and summer wildflowers begins. The forests have their own set of

flowers, less conspicuous and later in getting started, but nonetheless adding splashes of color to the forest floor.

The spruce-fir forests give way to more open forests of ponderosa pine near the North Rim, and finally to woodlands of pinyon and juniper at most places on the brink of the Canyon. The shift is due in part to decreasing elevation and in part to climatic effects of the Canyon itself, creating updrafts of warm, dry air from its depths. With the changes in forest type there are also changes in the kinds of plants found on the forest floor, adding to the variety of the display of wildflowers found in the park.

SOUTH RIM

The lower South Rim is too warm and dry in summer to support forests of spruce and fir, and even ponderosa pine is limited to protected sites on hillsides and along washes. The predominant vegetation of the South Rim is pinyon and juniper, forming

an open, low woodland very different from the forests of the North Rim. Snow often falls at the South Rim in winter, but accumulations are usually light and it often melts between storms. Spring wildflowers are abundant most years, gradually diminishing as the season progresses into the hot, dry days of June preceding the rains of summer. Starting in early July, afternoon thunderstorms frequently rumble over the Canyon rims, and the resultant moisture brings forth a second flowering season in summer. The abundance of summer flowers varies from year to year depending on the frequency and amount of moisture.

THE INNER CANYON

Below the rims, pinyon-juniper woodland prevails for the first few miles along the trails, the trees becoming smaller and more scattered with decreasing elevation. The Redwall Formation is the dividing point between woodland above and the shrubby high desert of the Tonto Plateau, 3000 feet below the South Rim. The grayish appearance of the Tonto is largely due to the nearly pure stands of evenly spaced blackbrush which grow there. Several other shrubs are also found there, and following wet winters a profusion of spring wildflowers carpets the ground with colorful displays.

The hottest, driest part of the Grand Canyon is the Inner Gorge, the area between the Tonto Plateau and the Colorado River in the central part of the Grand Canyon. A low-elevation hot desert plant community is found on the steep, often nearly vertical slopes of the Inner Gorge. Here summer temperatures often reach 40° C (115° F) and annual precipitation averages 210 mm (8.5 inches) at Phantom Ranch. The narrow corridor of desert along the Colorado River is really an eastern extension of the Mohave Desert. Paradoxically, the number of plant species found along the river is greatest near the Grand Wash Cliffs at the western end of the Grand Canyon since that is the area closest to the main part of the Mohave Desert. Cacti and various low shrubs predominate, and the Inner Gorge display of early spring wildflowers can be incredibly diverse providing sufficient rains have fallen during the winter.

SEGO LILY
Calochortus nuttallii
Lily family
Lilaceae

5

The sego lily, state flower of Utah, is commonly seen in flower in summer in the forests and woodlands of both rims. Generally the flowers are creamy white at Grand Canyon, although they vary from lilac to golden yellow in other areas. It is one of the most attractive wildflowers in the park. The bulbs were eaten in the past by Navajos and Hopis and by early pioneers in Utah in times of food scarcity. Like all other members of the Lily family, the sego lily is protected by law in Arizona. The species name honors Thomas Nuttall, an early nineteenth century naturalist who traveled widely in the West and described many species of plants and birds new to science.

Sego lilies have wide, cream-colored petals in contrast to the closely related weakstem mariposa lilies with their narrower pinkish or lavender petals. Sego lilies also have upright rather than spreading stems, and they are found mainly on the rims, while the weakstem mariposa blooms in spring and is confined to the Inner Canyon.

Grand Canyon 1995
June

SAND-VERBENA
Abronia elliptica

Four-o'clock family
Nyctaginaceae

Three species of sand-verbena are known to occur within the park. Depending on the species, flower color varies from white to pink or purplish-red. The white sand-verbena illustrated here is the most common, although it is confined to the Inner Canyon and is usually found on beaches along the Colorado River. During the day the plants are not especially conspicuous, but as evening approaches the flowers open, sending forth a sweet perfume that permeates the entire beach. The delicate scent lasts through the night, but as the first rays of sunlight reach the Inner Gorge the flowers close, saving moisture during the heat of the day. The flowers are pollinated by night-flying moths, attracted by the sweet-smelling nectar.

The perennial sand-verbena has a long root system reaching deep into the sand to obtain moisture. The round flower heads, each 5 to 8 cm (2 to 3 inches) in diameter, contain perhaps 30 individual flowers. Although the flowering season is concentrated in spring and early summer, a few flowers can sometimes be found along the river nearly any time during the year if conditions are favorable.

BANANA YUCCA
Yucca baccata
Lily family
Liliaceae

7

Of the five species of yucca in Grand Canyon National Park, banana yucca is the most common and widespread. It is found from the rims to the Tonto Plateau, and occasionally in the Inner Gorge. It is especially common on the South Rim. On the North Rim it is found only in dry habitats at the edge of the Canyon; it is absent from the moister, shady forest. Two other species of yucca (narrowleaf and Whipple yucca) replace it in the Inner Gorge.

Banana yucca flowers in the spring, producing a dense stalk of creamy white flowers from April in the Inner Canyon to June or July at higher elevations. The individual flowers are nearly spherical, and the outer flower parts are purplish. The common name refers to the large fleshy fruits appearing later in the summer. Several parts of the plant are used by southwestern

June
Grand Canyon 1995

Indians. The fruits are eaten raw, roasted, dried for winter use, ground into meal, or fermented to produce an alcoholic beverage. The leaves provide fiber for rope, mats, sandals, baskets, and cloth. The roots, known as amole, are used for soap and as a laxative. Pronubid moths lay their eggs in the ovary of the plant and in turn pollinate the flowers, ensuring development of the seeds on which the moth larvae feed.

Banana yucca is nearly stem-less, with the leaves clustered at or near the ground. The leaves are 40 to 75 cm (16 to 30 inches) long and about 5 cm (2 inches) wide with long, coarse fibers on the margins. The flowering stalk is 50 to 90 cm (20 to 36 inches) tall, barely surpassing the leaves and producing flowers nearly throughout its length. The much shorter, denser inflorescense with white instead of yellow flowers distinguish this plant from Utah agave when in flower. When

flowers are absent, the yucca with its fibrous leaf margins is easily distinguished from the agave which has hooked prickles on the edges of the leaves.

MINERS LETTUCE, INDIAN LETTUCE
Claytonia perfoliata
Portulaca family
Portulacaceae

9

One of the few members of the Portulaca family in Grand Canyon National Park, miners lettuce usually draws attention more by its large, bright green leaves than its flowers, which are very small. The plant is often encountered on moist, shaded banks or in crevices where seeps are found. It requires a rather reliable source of moisture. The photo was taken in April along the Bright Angel Trail below Indian Gardens.

As the common name indicates, the plant has been used as a salad plant and potherb by early settlers and Indians. The leaves are crisp and tasty when eaten fresh.

The upper two leaves are united in a saucer-like arrangement, termed perfoliate, and a cluster of small, white flowers arises from the center. The other leaves, which are usually numerous, are all basal. The tiny flowers are about 5 mm (1/5 inch) in diameter.

FENDLER SANDWORT
Arenaria fendleri

Pink family
Caryophyllaceae

Sunny, dry meadows on the North Rim are where Fendler sandwort may be seen in flower in July and August. One of the six species of sandwort in the park, its small white flowers are often overlooked. Some of the other species are found on the South Rim, as at Rowes Well, and on slopes and terraces of the Inner Canyon.

Sandworts have very narrow opposite leaves, appearing threadlike in Fendler sandwort and stiffly needlelike in some of the other species. The branched stems of Fendler sandwort are 3 to 30 cm (1 1/2 to 12 inches) long, and the plants are perennial. The five white petals are about 5 mm (1/4 inch) long. The plants furnish excellent forage but do not withstand heavy grazing.

PRICKLE-POPPY
Argemone munita
Poppy family
Papaveraceae

11

At about the time when most spring flowering plants are setting seed and most summer flowering plants are awaiting the first thunderstorm, prickle-poppy flowers begin to appear along the roadsides, in open fields and along the trails of the Inner Canyon. Prickle-poppies do well in disturbed places, and the large white flowers serve well in dressing up abandoned fields and roadsides. The prickly plants resemble thistles, and are often mistaken for them when flowers are not present, but they are not related.

Prickle-poppies are often abundant in overgrazed fields; their spininess and distastefulness, because they contain toxic alkaloids, make them unpalatable to livestock.

Several species of prickle-poppies are found in the Grand Canyon area. One species, which is quite rare, is known only from steep slopes in the Inner Canyon.

The flowers of all prickle-poppies are similar; the species differ mainly in the density of prickles on the stems and leaves. The stems are up to 1 m (3 feet) tall, and the flowers, mostly with 6 petals, are about 10 cm (4 inches) in diameter. The yellow in the center of the flower is the stamens, of which there may be up to 200. Flowering starts in April or May and may last into early fall, a rather lengthy season.

Grand Canyon June 1995

WATER-CRESS
Nasturtium officinale
Mustard family
Cruciferae

12

A native of Europe, water-cress is widely naturalized in North America and is found in the Grand Canyon along streams, in springs, and along the edge of shallow ponds. It grows along the Bright Angel Trail in Garden Creek below Indian Gardens, in Bright Angel Creek near Phantom Ranch, and along the Colorado River.

Excellent as a salad plant and a potherb, water-cress has been eaten and used medicinally for thousands of years. During Roman times it was considered food for deranged minds; Pliny listed 40 medicinal uses. The Greek physician Dioscorides warned that the seeds were bad for the stomach and spleen but expelled worms.

Water-cress is semiaquatic, usually found floating in shallow water or growing in mud. It has dense clusters of deeply divided dark green leaves. The inconspicuous white flowers, in clumps 12 mm (1/2 inch) across at the ends of the stems, appear from March through August.

Grand Canyon 1995 June

WILD CANDYTUFT, FENDLER PENNYCRESS
Thlaspi montanum

Mustard family
Cruciferae

SOUTH RIM
NORTH RIM
Flowers: March-August

13

Candytuft is one of the earliest spring wildflowers, appearing on the rims shortly after the snow melts. The small plants would go unnoticed later in the year, but they are a welcome harbinger of spring at a time when most plants are still dormant. Wild candytuft is often seen in March and April along the South Rim Trail, near the Visitor Center, and on the West Rim Trail. On the North Rim it flowers somewhat later, appearing in meadows in May and flowering as late as August in shaded canyons.

The individual plants of candytuft are small, with one or two flowering stalks usually less than 15 cm (6 inches) tall arising from a basal rosette of leaves. The plants often grow together in clumps, or the roots branch to form several rosettes. Numerous flowers, each with four white petals, appear at the top of the stalks, giving a clustered, tufted appearance to the plants.

NORTH RIM
INNER CANYON
Flowers: March-June

Fendlerbush is a showy shrub which is rather uncommon on the rims but is abundant a short distance below them in the Inner Canyon. It is especially abundant along the Bright Angel Trail from just below the South Rim to Indian Gardens, where the shrubs are covered with white flowers in April and May.

Fendlerbush is browsed by deer and bighorn sheep. Navajos reportedly smoked it, and used portions of the plant for ceremonial dishes.

Although not closely related, fendlerbush and Utah service-berry are easily confused. They are shrubs of similar habit, often growing together in the Grand Canyon. Distinguishing characters are the four petals per flower, narrow pointed leaves, and four-chambered woody capsules of fendlerbush,

contrasting with five petals per flower, rounded, toothed leaves, and small, fleshy, apple-like fruits of serviceberry.

The intricately branched shrubs are often 2 m (6 feet) tall. Occurring singly or in small clusters on the ends of the branches, the large flowers are about 25 mm (1 inch) in diameter.

14

UTAH SERVICEBERRY
Amelanchier utahensis

Rose family
Rosaceae

15

Serviceberry is an attractive shrub or small tree with its springtime dressing of white flowers. It is common in many areas of the park above 1200 m (4000 feet), especially close to the rims and along all of the Inner Canyon trails down to the Tonto Platform. Flowering starts in April at lower elevations, in May on the rims, and flowers are past in most areas by June.

One of the most valuable shrubs in the park for wildlife, serviceberry is browsed by deer and domestic livestock, and the small, apple-like fruits are important food sources for birds and other animals. The fruits may be eaten raw, cooked, or dried. Indians dried them and pounded them together in large loaves which remained sweet and were eaten after softening pieces in water or after placing pieces in soups or stews. Jam, jelly and wine may be made from the berries.

Serviceberry shrubs are 1 to 5 m (3 to 15 feet) tall with ovate leaves usually having several teeth toward the rounded tip. The numerous fragrant white flowers have five long, narrow petals and develop small apple-like fruits which are bluish-purple when ripe.

FERNBUSH
Chamaebatiaria millefolium
Rose family
Rosaceae

Delicate fernlike leaves are a distinctive characteristic separating fernbush from all other shrubs in Grand Canyon National Park. Flowering during August and September, fernbush is common on both rims. On the South Rim it is especially abundant in the campground and at the viewpoints along the East Rim Drive, particularly at Yaki Point.

Deer and sheep browse on fernbush leaves and stems; cattle apparently avoid it.

The shrubs grow up to 2 m (6 feet) tall; the finely dissected leaves are 2 to 4 cm (3/4 to 1 1/2 inch) long. The sticky, aromatic inflorescence, about 3 to 10 cm (1 to 4 inches) long, has numerous closely spaced white flowers at the ends of the branches.

CLIFFROSE
Cowania mexicana

Rose family
Rosaceae

17

A large, upright shrub covered with fragrant cream-colored flowers from April through September, cliffrose is an attractive member of the woodland plant community from the rims to the Tonto Platform. It is usually found in small openings in the pinyon-juniper woodland and is abundant on open, rocky slopes along the trails below the rims.

Cliffrose is closely related to and easily confused with Apache plume. The distinguishing characteristics are: cliffrose is more treelike, growing from a single trunk; its flowers are more yellowish; the leaves are waxy and dotted with glands but without hairs; and each flower produces 4 to 10 seeds with long, whitish plumose tails (styles). Apache plume is a shrub, much branched at the base; the flowers are white; the leaves lack glands and usually have short hairs; and the flowers produce about 25 purplish plumose styles.

June 1995
Grand Canyon

Various parts of cliffrose plants were used by Indians in the Southwest. The shredded bark was used to make clothing, sandals, mats and rope by native peoples in Utah and Nevada. The Hopis used the plant as an emetic and for washing wounds, and Navajos and Hopis both used the wood for arrows. The bitter-tasting foliage is an important winter browse for cattle, sheep and deer.

Cliffrose attains a height of 7.5 m (25 feet) in favorable habitats, sometimes forming "cliffrose forests" which are strikingly beautiful and over-whelmingly aromatic when the plants are in flower. The lower bark is shreddy and the leaves, with 3 to 5 deep lobes and narrow segments, are 6 to 15 mm (1/4 to 5/8 inch) long.

APACHE PLUME
Fallugia paradoxa
Rose family
Rosaceae

19

Growing as a much-branched, somewhat straggling shrub, Apache plume is especially common in dry washes on the rim, in small canyons below the rim, and at the old spring flood line along much of the Colorado River. Sometimes it grows along roadsides in open places on the rims, occasionally with the similar-appearing cliffrose. The pure white flowers of Apache plume appear in spring, starting in April in the Inner Gorge and in June on the rims, and may reappear in early fall. The large, purplish globose fruits appear soon after flowering. The styles, arising from the end of each individual seed, elongate to 25 to 50 mm (1 to 2 inches), forming a fuzzy cluster.

The stems were used for arrows by some Indians, while the Hopi used an infusion of the leaves to promote hair growth. It also serves to stabilize the banks of normally dry washes during flash floods.

Frequently forming dense clumps, the shrubs are from 30 to 150 cm (1 to 5 feet) tall. The five-petaled flowers are 2.5 to 5 cm (1 to 2 inches) across, and the leaves, with 3 to 7 linear lobes, are 5 to 20 mm (1/4 to 3/4 inches) long.

WILD STRAWBERRY
Fragaria ovalis
Rose family
Rosaceae

NORTH RIM
Flowers: June-July

Wild strawberries in Grand Canyon National Park are found mainly in the moister meadows and deep forests of the North Rim. Flowering in June and July, and fruiting several weeks later, they are a treasure confined to the higher elevations. The strawberry, actually a fleshy red enlargement of the base (receptacle) on which the flower is borne, contains numerous seeds which pass unharmed through the digestive tract of animals that relish them and inadvertently disperse the seeds.

Although the berries are small, they are sweet and juicy and provide a delicious morsel for birds and other animals, including hikers who happen upon them.

Wild strawberries also spread by runners (stolons) which root at the nodes and start new plants. The white flowers have five rounded petals and are 15 to 25 mm (1/2 to 1 inch) across. The fruits are 8 to 15 mm (1/4 to 1/2 inch) long. Each leaf consists of three leaflets, rounded and toothed at the apex.

ROCKMAT
Petrophytum caespitosum

Rose family
Rosaceae

21

Although actually a woody plant, rockmat has many very short branched stems with rosettes of closely spaced leaves, forming mats on bare rock surfaces. Growing from crevices in the bedrock, rockmat is often the last plant seen at the very brink of the Canyon and often grows on vertical cliffs where cracks afford it a foothold. It is common on both rims, and may be seen near the start of the West Rim Trail. In the Inner Gorge it occurs only in seeps, often growing on active travertine surfaces where water is always available. Its dense spikes of delicate light pink flowers appear in summer and early fall.

The flat dense plants, hugging the rock surface, appear almost mosslike from a distance. The mats may become 30 to 60 cm (1 to 2 feet) across and the flowering stalks grow 3 to 10 cm (1 to 4 inches) tall. The plants grow very slowly and may live for many years.

WHITE CRANESBILL, WHITE GERANIUM

Geranium richardsonii

Geranium family
Geraniaceae

A summer flowering plant at high elevations in the park, white cranesbill is common along roadsides in forested areas of the North Rim. Greenland Spring, the Cape Royal Road and the Point Sublime Road are good places to see it. A plant mainly found in spruce-fir forests, it is replaced on the South Rim by purple cranesbill.

A perennial herb, white cranesbill has stems 30 to 90 cm (12 to 36 inches) tall, mostly branched above the base. The five-petaled white flowers are about 2.5 cm (1 inch) across, and the leaves are sharply cut into five lobes.

PALE HOPTREE
Ptelea trifoliata

Rue family
Rutaceae

23

A large shrub or small tree, pale hoptree occurs in the Inner Canyon above the Tonto Plateau, and is often seen in open canyons in the lower part of the woodland zone. A good place to see the plant is along the Bright Angel Trail just below Indian Gardens.

The leaves are three-parted and have a pungent, citrus-like smell when crushed. The strong odor apparently keeps livestock from browsing the plants. The wafer-like fruits reportedly have been used in brewing as a substitute for hops (hence the common name) and in making bread.

Growing up to 6 m (20 feet) tall, the trees are covered with clusters of pendant, white flowers in April and May. Each flower has four or five narrow, rounded petals 4 to 7 mm (1/8 to 1/4 inch) long and the same number of conspicuous yellow-tipped stamens. The flat fruits are 1 to 2 cm (3/8 to 3/4 inch) in diameter. Shiny and dotted with tiny glands, the pointed leaves are 2 to 7 cm (3/4 to 2 3/4 inches) long.

GREASEBUSH
Forsellesia nevadensis
Crossosoma family
Crossosomataceae

A much-branched, somewhat spiny shrub, greasebush is common along the upper sections of the Inner Canyon trails and in Toroweap Valley. It is most likely to be encountered between the rim and the Supai Formation where large numbers of shrubby species and pinyon and juniper occur. Inconspicuous most of the year, the bushes are covered with attractive small white flowers from early April through May. The plants are important as browse for sheep and deer.

The intricately branched shrubs grow up to 2 m (6 1/2 feet) tall but are usually much smaller. The flower, about 10 mm (3/8 inch) in diameter, has five waxy, pointed petals and a greenish center. The leaves are oblong in shape, 5 to 12 mm (1/4 to 1/2 inch) long.

24

WHITE TUFTED EVENING-PRIMROSE

Oenothera caespitosa

Evening-primrose family
Onagraceae

25

Flowering from May through the summer on both rims, this evening-primrose is a conspicuous sight along roadsides and in open areas. The large white flowers open in evening, after the heat of day is past, and close soon after the sun hits them the next morning. Each flower lasts just one night, turning pink as it wilts. There are a number of evening-primroses in the park, some with yellow flowers, some with upright stems, and some with much smaller flowers. Of the two white-flowered stemless species, this one has the largest flowers; the other one (*Oenothera cavernae*) is found only in the Inner Canyon.

Night-flying insects pollinate the fragrant blossoms. The adaptation to blooming at night reduces water loss through the flowers during the day, since the flowering season is often the hottest, driest part of the year.

Leaves and flowers all arise directly from the root crown. The flowers, with their four notched white petals, may be 7 1/2 cm (3 inches) in diameter. The many leaves, covered with velvet-like hairs, are variously toothed and are 3 to 10 cm (1 1/4 to 4 inches) long on a petiole nearly as long. Rarely the plants develop a stem up to 20 cm (8 inches) long.

Grand Canyon June 1995

FLOWERING ASH
Fraxinus cuspidata var. *macropetala*
Olive family
Oleaceae

Of the five species of ash in Arizona, three of which occur in the park, this is the only one which has showy flowers. This fragrant small tree is not very common, but its beauty in flower makes it well worth searching for. It occurs at the top of the Redwall Limestone on east or north facing slopes in side canyons off the West Rim Drive. The Dripping Springs Trail in late May is perhaps the best place to see it in flower.

Most ashes have inconspicuous flowers lacking petals; this species is very unusual in its showiness and its fragrant flowers. The trees (or sometimes shrubs) are 1 to 7 m (3 to 23 feet) tall, covered with pendant groups of flowers with four narrow white petals about 10 mm (3/8 inch) long. The fruits have wings about 12 mm (1/2 inch) long. Its compound leaves have 3 to 7 leaflets, mostly less than 4 cm (1 1/2 inches) long.

FIELD BINDWEED, MORNING-GLORY
Convolvulus arvensis

Morning-glory family
Convolvulaceae

27

An introduced species especially common in abandoned fields and along roadsides, field bindweed is found in disturbed areas in Grand Canyon Village and elsewhere on the rims. The plants are trailing or twining vines with round white flowers. A native of Europe, field bindweed is considered a noxious weed which is difficult to eradicate in agricultural areas. Large patches are actually rather pretty with their multitude of flowers appearing from May to September.

The prostrate stems, rooting at the nodes, vary from 20 to 120 cm (8 to 48 inches) in length. The round, open funnel-shaped flowers are 15 to 25 mm (5/8 to 1 inch) across, usually with pinkish bands on the underside. The leaves are variable but are usually oblong and 1 to 5 cm (3/8 to 2 inches) long.

BRISTLY HIDDENFLOWER
Cryptantha setosissima

Borage family
Boraginaceae

Cryptantha is one of the largest genera of plants in the park, with about 25 species. Some of them are rather large, coarse biennials or perennials, found mostly on the rims and at higher elevations in the Inner Canyon; the others are small, delicate annuals common in the Inner Gorge.

Bristly hiddenflower is a perennial and is the tallest member of the genus in the park. It is found on both rims, often along roadsides in the pine belt, flowering from May to September.

Growing up to 1 m (3 1/4 feet) tall, the course plants are very bristly, almost spiny to the touch. The flower clusters vary from very short to half the length of the stem. The individual flowers are about 1 cm (3/8 inch) across with a light yellow center.

SACRED DATURA
Datura meteloides
Potato family
Solanaceae

29

The large funnelform flowers of sacred datura, along with its large leaves, are hard to miss along the Bright Angel Trail at Indian Gardens, at Phantom Ranch, and at various other Inner Canyon localities. The white flowers, largest of any in the park, open at night and wilt as soon as the sun hits them, turning them purple or brown. Although the flowering season is mainly in the summer, in the Inner Gorge the flowers may appear in spring. Nearly as unusual as the flowers are the large, round, spiny capsuled fruits resembling horse-chestnuts.

All parts of the plant are poisonous, containing various alkaloids, notably atropine. Humans as well as livestock have been poisoned and occasionally killed from eating sacred datura. Indians used its narcotic properties to induce visions, a dangerous practice which can easily lead to serious illness, blindness, or death.

The plants are perennial with erect, widely branching stems 50 to 180 cm (20 to 70 inches) long. The flowers, with united petals, are 15 to 25 cm (6 to 10 inches) long and 10 to 20 cm (4 to 8 inches) wide. Very prickly capsules 3 to 4 cm (1 1/4 to 1 1/2 inches) in diameter develop from the flowers. The oval or heart-shaped velvety leaves are 4 to 15 cm (1 1/2 to 6 inches) long.

DESERT TOBACCO
Nicotiana trigonophylla

Potato family
Solanaceae

Flowering nearly any time of the year in its favored Inner Gorge habitat, desert tobacco is a tall, glandular, white-flowered biennial or perennial. Another species, coyote tobacco, is very similar in appearance and is more common at higher elevations.

The leaves of desert tobacco contain nicotine and are smoked by some Indians on ceremonial occasions. Although animals usually avoid the plant, cases of poisoning in domestic livestock have been reported.

Growing 20 to 90 cm (8 to 36 inches) tall, desert tobacco produces a loose inflorescence on the upper parts of the stems. The flowers have an elongate narrow tube formed from the fused petals, 12 to 22 mm (1/2 to 7/8 inch) long. The sticky, glandular leaves are 5 to 15 cm (2 to 6 inches) long and 1 to 4 cm (3/8 to 1 1/2 inches) wide.

Grand Canyon June 1995

DESERT BEDSTRAW
Galium stellatum
Madder family
Rubiaceae

31

This species of bedstraw is a low, much-branched shrub with woody lower stems and herbaceous upper parts. It is common in desert areas on dry, rocky slopes below the Tonto Plateau in the Inner Gorge. Notable features include the sharp-pointed small, stiff leaves in groups of four, and the myriad of very tiny flowers. Male and female parts are in separate flowers, and while most individuals have some of each, either male or female flowers seem to predominate on a plant. The male flowers are minute and greenish with four petals, while the female flowers are so small that only the fuzzy ovary is readily visible. In fruit, the female plants have the appearance of being covered with innumerable fuzzy ornaments.

Bedstraw plants are 20 to 70 cm (8 to 28 inches) tall. The profusely branched stems have shreddy gray bark at the base. The narrow leaves are 3 to 10 mm (1/8 to 3/8 inch) long with a rough, sandpaper-like surface. The fruits, including the speading white hairs, are 3 to 4 mm (1/8 inch) in diameter. Bedstraw is rather inconspicuous at a distance, but shows unusual beauty upon close inspection.

Grand Canyon June 1995

BLUEBERRY ELDER
Sambucus glauca

Honeysuckle family
Caprifoliaceae

A large shrub or small tree, blueberry elder may be seen flowering in June, July and August at Cape Royal, Bright Angel Spring, on the North Kaibab Trail and at Grandview Point. A large elderberry has been planted just west of Bright Angel Lodge. Flat-topped clusters of many small white flowers appear at the ends of the branches, developing into dark blue berries covered with a whitish bloom.

The berries are an important food source for wildlife, especially birds. The foliage is browsed by domestic animals and deer. The fruit is rather tart when eaten raw but can be made into fine jelly, pies, and wine, and the bark and leaves are reputed to have medicinal value as a purgative.

Blueberry elder plants grow 2 to 8 m (6 1/2 to 26 feet) tall. The inflorescence is 5 to 20 cm (2 to 8 inches) across and rather dense with flowers. Each flower potentially develops into a single berry about 6 mm (1/4 inch) in diameter. The leaves are compound with five to nine lance-shaped, toothed leaflets.

32

Grand Canyon June 1995

WESTERN YARROW
Achillea millefolium

Sunflower family
Compositae

33

Finely divided fern-like leaves and a flat-topped cluster of many small white flowers characterize western yarrow. The species is adapted to grow in a diversity of habitats but apparently is fairly rare in the park except on the North Rim. It is found there flowering from June through September in many places, including the entrance station, Greenland Spring, Cape Royal Road, and the North Rim Ranger Station. Ponderosa pine forests and sunny meadows are its favored locations.

Yarrow has a long history of medicinal use. Indians used the dried leaves to stop bleeding of wounds and to heal inflammation. Boiled in water as a tea, the plant was given for indigestion, toothache, or generally run-down health. It was widely used in family medicine among early Arizona settlers. The crushed leaves have a distinctive odor and a minty taste.

The densely hairy plants grow 25 to 50 cm (10 to 20 inches) tall with a terminal flower cluster. The leaves are 3 to 10 cm (1 1/4 to 4 inches) long and 15 mm (5/8 inch) wide or less. The plants are widely distributed in western North America and are closely related to the European yarrow, used medicinally since ancient times.

WHITE ASTER
Leucelene ericoides
Sunflower family
Compositae

This small white woodland aster is certainly not as conspicuous as some of its cousins. However, it is often encountered in the vicinity of Grand Canyon Village and along the East Rim Drive into the sagebrush desert. Flowering in April and May, and again in late summer if the rainfall is sufficient, the plants produce white flowers on the numerous short stems arising from branching woody roots.

The stems, 6 to 12 cm (2 3/8 to 4 3/4 inches) tall, have many closely spaced narrow leaves, mostly 1 cm (3/8 inch) long or less. The flowers are about 15 mm (5/8 inch) across.

Grand Canyon June 1995

SEEPWILLOW
Baccharis salicifolia
Sunflower family
Compositae

35

Not a true willow at all, seepwillow gets its name from its willow-like growth form and its favored habitat along streams and washes. In the Grand Canyon it occurs along the Colorado River throughout the length of the Canyon, and is found up side canyons which have running water. Along the Bright Angel Trail it is first encountered at Indian Gardens; it is abundant along Hermit Creek on the lower part of the Hermit Trail, and along Bright Angel Creek for a long distance upstream from the Colorado. The delicate white flowers, appearing almost any time of year except mid-winter, are clustered at the ends of the branches.

The plant has been used as a remedy for chills; an infusion of the aromatic, sticky leaves has been used as an eyewash, and some Indians chewed the twigs to alleviate toothache. In Mexico the stems are placed under tiles on roofs and used as temporary thatching.

Seepwillow often grows in clumps or thickets with stems 1 to 5 m (3 to 16 feet) tall.

Male and female flowers are on different plants. After flowering, the female plants produce myriads of seeds with silky tails, allowing them to disperse in the wind. The leaves are lance-shaped, with three prominent parallel veins and a waxy, shiny covering that imparts a distinctive odor to the shrub and sometimes permeates an area where thickets of seepwillow grow. The leaves have several large teeth on each side and are 5 to 12 cm (2 to 4 3/4 inches) long.

Grand Canyon June 1995

DESERT BRICKELL-BUSH
Brickellia atractyloides
Sunflower family
Compositae

A small, much-branched shrub of the Inner Canyon, desert brickell-bush is found on sunny, rocky slopes and is most common in the Inner Gorge. It may be seen along the trails below the Tonto Plateau. The rather distinctive leaves are pointed and spiny-toothed with very prominent veins in a net-like pattern on both sides. Small pinkish flowering heads without obvious petals appear on the plants from March to June.

Desert brickell-bush is well adapted to very dry conditions and retains most of its leaves during all but the severest dry spells.

The intricately branched shrubs grow 20 to 30 cm (8 to 12 inches) tall, shedding the bark of older twigs in long shreds. The heads, actually containing about 50 tiny individual flowers, are 10 to 13 mm (3/8 to 1/2 inch) across. The stiff leaves are about 5 to 15 mm (1/4 to 5/8 inch) long. Desert brickell-bush is a good example of a plant that has

migrated up the desert corridor of the Inner Gorge from the hot deserts west of the Grand Canyon.

WHEELER THISTLE
Cirsium wheeleri

Sunflower family
Compositae

37

Flowering from July to October, Wheeler thistle has either purple-lavender or white flowers. It is perhaps the most common thistle on both rims. The white form is often encountered on the North Rim. The large, prickly plants are unmistakable as thistles but it is difficult to distinguish between some of the ten species found in the park. The Navajos and Hopis reportedly use thistles medicinally for various disorders.

Wheeler thistle stems are 40 to 80 cm (16 to 32 inches) tall. The stems are branched in the upper part, and the spiny flowering heads are usually solitary at the ends of the branches and are 2 to 3 cm (3/4 to 1 1/4 inch) high. The leaves are deeply divided and each of the lobes is armed with slender spines. The upper surface of the leaves is green, and the lower surface is white with dense, woolly hairs.

Grand Canyon 1995 June

HAIRY FLEABANE
Erigeron concinnus
Sunflower family
Compositae

Hairy fleabane is a small daisy-like flower found from the upper parts of the Inner Canyon to the rims. Flowering from April to October, it may be seen in Grand Canyon Village, at Hermits Rest, along the Kaibab and Bright Angel Trails below the South Rim, and on Walhalla Plateau on the North Rim. There are thirteen different kinds of fleabane in the park, some of which are very difficult to distinguish. Spreading fleabane *(Erigeron divergens)* is very similar to hairy fleabane except that it is annual rather than perennial and starts flowering later on the rims.

The plants have a central taproot branched at the top producing many leafy stems 10 to 50 cm (4 to 20 inches) tall. The flowers, with 50 to 100 white petals (rays) and yellow centers, are about 25 to 35 mm (1 to 1 3/8 inches) across. The narrow leaves are about 20 to 40 mm (3/4 to 1 1/2 inches) long and, like the stems, are densely hairy.

Grand Canyon June 1995

STEMLESS TOWNSENDIA
Townsendia exscapa
Sunflower family
Compositae

39

This is one of the earliest of spring wildflowers in the park. This small perennial produces several large flower heads soon after warm weather replaces snow on the rims. Seemingly outsized for such a small plant, the heads with their white petals and light yellow centers sometimes nearly cover the plants. Stemless townsendia may be seen in Grand Canyon Village and along the South Rim Trail flowering in March and April, and on the North Rim in late May and June.

The plants are completely stemless, with leaves and flowers arising directly from the root crown. The leaves, grayish in color with sparse hairs, are narrow and crowded, about 1 to 5 cm (3/8 to 2 inches) long. The flowering heads are 15 to 25mm (5/8 to 1 inch) in diameter.

Brittlebush

UTAH AGAVE
Agave utahensis

Amaryllis family
Amaryllidaceae

41

Utah agave is one of the most widespread plants in the park. It is common in open, rocky places on both rims and is found all the way to the river, growing in some incredibly hot and dry places on the schist of the Inner Gorge. Its wide elevational range is unusual, as there are few plants found both on the rims and along the river. Like cacti (to which they are not related), agaves store water in their succulent parts, in this case leaves rather than stems. Agaves are often called century plants because many years pass before the flowering stalk appears. The life span is 15-25 years rather than a century, however, and the plants die after flowering once.

Early Indian inhabitants of the Canyon roasted agaves for food in so-called "mescal pits," from the Spanish name for the plant. The circular pits of loose stone are among the most common archeological remains in the Inner Canyon.

The plants grow in clusters of several rosettes, except for the Kaibab agave subspecies which grows singly. The fleshy leaves are 15 to 35 cm (6 to 15 inches) long, tapering to a sharp point, and 2 to 5 cm (1 to 2 inches) wide, with hooked spines on the edges. The stalks are 1 to 4 m (3 to 14 feet) or more tall, and the numerous yellow flowers are arranged in a narrow spike along the upper two-thirds of the stalk. Flowering time varies from early May in the Inner Gorge to late July on the North Rim.

Grand Canyon 1995 June

GOLDEN WILD-BUCKWHEAT
Eriogonum corymbosum

Buckwheat family
Polygonaceae

At least 23 species of wild-buckwheat are found in Grand Canyon National Park; 51 are known to occur in Arizona. Although the genus exhibits a great variety of growth forms, many of the species are difficult to distinguish. Some are annuals with leaves only at the base and an intricately branched inflorescence (skeleton-weeds), while others are shrubs like golden wild-buckwheat. Flower colors vary from white to red and yellow.

This species was photographed near Point Sublime where the plants were literally covered with dense clumps of bright yellow flowers in August. The shrubby buckwheats are most common on the rims, flowering following summer rains, while the annual species are most often found flowering in the Inner Canyon in spring.

The cultivated buckwheat is in a closely related genus (*Fagopyrum*). Wild-buckwheats are an important nectar source for honeybees in areas where they are especially abundant, and the seeds serve as food for birds and rodents.

DESERT-TRUMPET
Eriogonum inflatum
Buckwheat family
Polygonaceae

43

With its inflated stems and branched inflorescence, desert-trumpet is a striking plant which attracts the attention of most Canyon hikers. It may be seen along the Inner Canyon trails on dry, rocky slopes from just below the rims to the Colorado River. The inflation of the stems is a structural adaptation for support. On small plants only the lower segment of the stem is inflated, but on larger plants three or more levels of stems may be affected.

The inflated portion is always the upper part of a stem segment just below the point of branching.

Tiny yellow flowers appear in large numbers on threadlike stalks at the ultimate divisions of the stems. The plants may be seen in flower nearly throughout the warm months, from late March through October, and the dried stems persist through the winter. With sufficient moisture the stems may grow 80 cm (30 inches) tall. The shiny, roundish leaves are all at the base of the plant.

HEART-LEAF BUTTERCUP
Ranunculus cardiophyllus

Buttercup family
Ranunculaceae

Flowering from June through August, heartleaf buttercup is most commonly found in the park-like meadows of the North Rim. It is probably the most abundant of the buttercups in the park, and favors the driest habitat of the eight species found here. Most of the other buttercups are found in marshy areas near the small lakes and springs on the North Rim, and some can be seen along streams on the edge of the forest. Although seldom seen on the South Rim, where the early summer is too hot and dry and natural ponds and marshes are absent, there are several species of buttercups found in the Inner Gorge along the shores of the Colorado River.

Buttercups as a group are poisonous, and the active ingredient, anemonal, is reputed to be a cardiac poison. The acrid juice causes inflammation and blisters if applied to the skin. The species vary in degree of toxicity; the most poisonous species, bitter buttercup (*Ranunculus sceleratus*) has been reported from the Grand Canyon only once, along the Colorado River at the far western end of the Canyon. The toxin is volatile and is rendered harmless by sufficient boiling or drying.

Heart-leaf buttercup is so named because of the shape of the basal leaves. The shiny yellow flowers are rather large for buttercups, 2 to 3 cm (3/4 to 1 1/2 inches) across. The plants are 15 to 40 cm (6 to 15 inches) tall and are common throughout the Rocky Mountains, reaching their southern limit in northern New Mexico and Arizona.

44

GOLDEN CORYDALIS
Corydalis aurea
Poppy family
Papaveraceae

45

Although one would never know it by looking at the asymmetrical flowers, golden corydalis is a member of the poppy family. A low, much branched perennial herb, it is found at scattered locations on the rims, such as Horsethief Tank on the South Rim where it flowers in May and June, and in protected spots in the Inner Gorge where it flowers somewhat earlier. The plants produce copious numbers of rich golden-yellow flowers.

The flowers are 12 to 15 mm (about 1/2 inch) long with a short spur giving them an irregular shape. The leaves of golden corydalis are slightly succulent and are deeply divided. The plants contain poisonous alkaloids which are especially toxic during early spring. Dutchman's breeches, a common spring woodland flower in the eastern United States, and the cultivated bleeding-heart, are closely related to golden corydalis.

WESTERN WALLFLOWER
Erysimum asperum
Mustard family
Cruciferae

The showiest of the many members of the Mustard family in the park is western wallflower. Its dense heads of bright yellow or yellow-orange flowers are a common sight in Grand Canyon Village, at Yavapai Point, and along East and West Rim Drives from May into July. The plants flower on the North Rim from June to August, and in the Inner Canyon down to the Tonto Plateau in April.

Native Americans used the plant for a variety of medicinal purposes, including treatment of sunburn and respiratory congestion. It is probably used occasionally as a browse plant by elk, deer, and bighorn sheep.

Western wallflower is a biennial or perennial up to 80 cm (32 inches) tall. The leaves are concentrated at the base and the lower half of the stem. The stems elongate after flowering, producing long, narrow, upright pods. The individual flowers with their four broad petals are about 1.5 cm (1/2 inch) in diameter.

46

PRINCE'S-PLUME, DESERT-PLUME
Stanleya pinnata
Mustard family
Cruciferae

47

A conspicuous spring and early summer flowering plant in the Inner Canyon, prince's-plume is the largest member of the Mustard family in the Grand Canyon. It is found on steep, rocky slopes along most of the trails below the rims. Its showy wands of yellow flowers are also a familiar sight along the Colorado River throughout the Grand Canyon.

The tender stems and leaves of prince's-plume have a cabbage-like taste. The seeds may be parched, ground, and eaten as mush. However, large amounts of prince's-plume are likely to be poisonous because the plant accumulates toxic selenium from the soil, incorporating it in place of sulfur in the production of amino acids.

Branching only at the base of the plant, the stems of prince's-plume are 40 to 150 cm (16 to 60 inches) tall. The upper half of the stalks is covered with an elongate plume of many yellow flowers. The four narrow petals are each about 12 to 16 mm (1/2 to 5/8 inch) long. The large leaves are simple or divided into long narrow segments.

Grand Canyon June 1995

CINQUEFOIL
Potentilla osterhoutii
Rose family
Rosaceae

SOUTH RIM
NORTH RIM
INNER CANYON
Flowers: June-September

Eight different species of cinquefoil have been identified in Grand Canyon National Park; 20 species of this complex genus occur in Arizona. One species (rare in the park) is shrubby, but most are upright herbs with palmately lobed leaves. While neither the showiest nor most widespread species in the park, the little plant pictured here is often seen in the vicinity of Grand Canyon Village. In July and August, it may be seen flowering along the West Rim

Trail a short distance from Bright Angel Lodge, growing in cracks in vertical faces of Kaibab Limestone outcrops. It is perhaps more widespread on the North Rim, where it occurs at Cape Royal, Point Sublime, and several less accessible places, growing as a mat in rock crevices.

All of the Grand Canyon species have five yellow (rarely whitish) petals, the flowers resembling a yellow wild strawberry or wild rose. This species has smaller flowers than most, about 10 mm (3/8 inch) across, in small clusters. The leaves have 5 to 11 rounded glandular-sticky leaflets which are shallowly lobed.

UTAH DEERVETCH
Lotus utahensis

Pea family
Leguminosae

49

Low, straggling herbs might best describe deervetch, but what they lack in distinctiveness as plants they more than compensate by their colorful red and yellow flowers. Two very closely related species are found in the park. Utah deervetch is more common on the North Rim and Wrights deervetch (*Lotus wrightii*) is usually seen on the South Rim. Both are much-branched perennial herbs.

The common name comes from the utilization of the plants as browse by deer. Navajos considered Wrights deervetch as a Life Medicine used to heal injuries and have used it to relieve digestive problems.

Utah deervetch stems are 10 to 30 cm (4 to 12 inches) long, and the flowers, in groups of one to three, are 10 to 15 mm (3/8 to 5/8 inch) long. Each leaf has three to seven small, very narrow leaflets.

YELLOW SWEET-CLOVER
Melilotus officinalis
Pea family
Leguminosae

A tall bushy annual or perennial, yellow sweet-clover is found along roadsides and in open, often disturbed areas on the rims. It is also fairly common along the shores of the Colorado River. Flowering on the rims in summer and early fall, and along the river most of the year, yellow sweet-clover and the closely related white sweet-clover often grow together and are very similar except for the flower color. Both were introduced from Eurasia. The sweet clovers are excellent honey plants and are favorite browse for mule deer.

Sweet-clover plants may grow nearly 2 m (6 1/2 feet) tall. The small flowers, about 6 mm (1/4 inch) long, are in dense elongate spikes at the ends of the branches. The leaves are compound with three leaflets 10 to 20 mm (3/8 to 3/4 inch) long.

50

Grand Canyon June 1995

GOLDEN PEA
Thermopsis rhombifolia
Pea family
Leguminosae

51

One of the earlier spring-flowering plants, golden pea is found scattered on the rims, mainly in ponderosa pine forests. Its flowering season is from early April to June. Golden pea somewhat resembles the lupines, but has only three leaflets and fewer flowers in a more open inflorescence; also, none of the lupines have such bright yellow flowers.

Golden pea sometimes forms patches through spreading of its rootstocks. The upright stems grow 30 to 60 cm (12 to 24 inches) tall, and the flowers, in a terminal cluster surpassing the leaves, are each 15 to 25 mm (5/8 to 1 inch) long. The leaflets point upward and are 3 to 8 cm (1 to 3 inches) long.

STICKLEAF
Mentzelia pumila
Loasa family
Loasaceae

INNER CANYON
TOROWEAP
Flowers: March-September

One of the spring flowers of the Inner Canyon, stickleaf is a biennial commonly found on slopes and terraces from the Colorado River to the rims. It has large ten-petaled yellow flowers, and the many yellow stamens give the waxy flowers a cactus-like appearance.

The name stickleaf arises from the short barbed hairs on the leaves, which make them adhere to clothing if one brushes against them. The leaves feel like sandpaper to the touch. Other members of the family in the tropics have stinging hairs on the stems and leaves which may inflict painful injury.

The tortuous, branched stems of stickleaf are about 20 to 45 cm (8 to 18 inches) long with yellowish-white peeling epidermis on the older parts. The flowers are about 20 to 40 mm (3/4 to 1 1/2 inches) in diameter with 60 to 120 stamens. The dark green, shiny leaves are 10 to 40 mm (3/8 to 1 1/2 inches) or more long with sinuous margins.

52

DESERT PRICKLY-PEAR CACTUS
Opuntia phaeacantha

Cactus family
Cactaceae

53

Found mostly below the Supai Formation, this prickly-pear has pink or yellow flowers. The photograph was taken at Phantom Ranch in April. Like grizzly-bear cactus it is a prostrate plant with branches spreading along the ground and rooting where they make contact.

The pads of this prickly-pear measure 15 to 25 or more cm (6 to 10 inches) in length and 7.5 to 22.5 cm (3 to 9 inches) in width.

Spines are fewer in number than on grizzly-bear, are confined mostly to the upper half or two-thirds of the pads, and are 2.5 to 5 cm (1 to 2 inches) in length. The large flowers, often tinged with red at the base, are 6 to 11 cm (2 1/2 to 3 1/4 inches) in diameter. The fleshy fruits are purplish at maturity and are sweet and edible raw (after the spines are removed), cooked, or in jam.

Grand Canyon June 1995

WHIPPLE CHOLLA
Opuntia whipplei
Cactus family
Cactaceae

SOUTH RIM
NORTH RIM
INNER CANYON
INNER GORGE
Flowers: May-August

Perhaps the most widely distributed cactus in the Grand Canyon, Whipple cholla is found from both rims to the Colorado River, and occasionally throughout the length of the Inner Canyon. Its unusual greenish flowers appear in May at low elevations and from June through August on the rims. Dripping Springs Trail and Desert View are good places to see Whipple cholla.

Hopis boiled the fleshy yellow fruits and ate them with squash. March was sometimes called the "cactus moon" because this cholla was often the only vegetable food available at that time of year.

In the Grand Canyon, Whipple cholla is usually low and bushy or mat forming, growing 30 to 60 cm (1 to 2 feet) tall. The joints are 7.5 to 15 cm (3 to 6 inches) long. The greenish or yellowish-green flowers are 2 to 3 cm (3/4 to 1 1/4 inches) across, and the fleshy fruits are yellow at maturity.

54

TALL YELLOW EVENING-PRIMROSE
Oenothera longissima

Evening-primrose family
Onagraceae

55

Found mostly along roadsides on the North Rim, tall yellow evening-primrose has flowers which open in the evening and wilt by mid-morning, the petals turning orange-red with age. Two species of tall yellow evening-primrose occur in the park, overlapping somewhat in their distribution. This species has long (8 to 12 cm; 3 1/4 to 4 3/4 inches) floral tubes beneath the yellow petals. The other species (*Oenothera hookeri*) has floral tubes 2.5 to 5 cm (1 to 2 inches)

long. The latter species is fairly common on sandy beaches along the Colorado River as well as at lower elevations on the rims.

A biennial or short-lived perennial, tall yellow evening-primrose has upright stems 1 to 3 m (3 to 10 feet) tall. Its four yellow petals are about 4 cm (1 1/2 inches) long and the flowers are about 6 to 8 cm (2 1/2 to 4 1/4 inches) in diameter.

THICK-LEAVED GROUNDCHERRY
Physalis crassifolia

Potato family
Solanaceae

Dime-sized round yellow flowers and succulent leaves characterize this Inner Gorge spring-flowering herb. Found in some of the hottest, driest places in the Canyon, groundcherry is a perennial herb well adapted to living in the desert, where it is often seen on the talus slopes of the Inner Gorge schist.

The stems are spreading-branched forming a compact plant. The flowers are 10 to 15 mm (3/8 to 5/8 inch) across, round in outline with joined petals. In fruit the sepals enlarge, becoming inflated and enclosing the round, green berry. The oval leaves are mostly 15 to 35 mm (5/8 to 1 3/8 inches) long.

YELLOW MONKEYFLOWER
Mimulus guttatus
Figwort family
Scrophulariaceae

57

Although fairly limited in its occurrence at Grand Canyon, yellow monkeyflower is widely distributed elevationally and geographically throughout the West. Its yellow flowers with red spots resembling a monkey face give the plant its common name. In the Grand Canyon it has been recorded along Bright Angel Creek near Phantom Ranch, and at other side canyon localities in the Inner Gorge.

The plants may be eaten raw as salad greens or cooked as potherbs. They have a slightly bitter flavor.

With stems 5 to 100 cm (2 to 39 inches) tall, the perennial plants nearly always grow in clumps in or adjacent to small streams. Shady side canyons and permanently flowing seeps are their preferred habitat. The flowers are about 2.5 cm (1 inch) long, with petals fused in a short tube, then flaring outward

broadly. If the stems topple over, roots will develop where they touch soil. The heavily veined leaves are usually oval and are paired along the stems.

WOOLLY MULLEIN
Verbascum thapsus
Figwort family
Scrophulariaceae

A conspicuous biennial common on the rims, woolly mullein develops a basal rosette of densely hairy leaves the first year. It sends up a tall flowering stalk the second year, after which the plant dies. Naturalized from Europe, it is a common weed along roadsides, in disturbed areas, and sometimes in the forest.

In the Mediterranean region, **where** woolly mullein is native, the leaves are gathered for use in making lotions to soften the skin and in making medicines to soothe inflamed tissues. The seeds, available on the stalks sticking above the snow, are a source of winter food for small birds.

The stout stems grow 30 to 200 cm (1 to 6 1/2 feet) tall, producing flowers more than half their length in a dense, elongate spike. Individual yellow flowers are 15 to 25 mm (1/2 to 1 inch)

wide, appearing from July through September. The large woolly basal leaves, 10 to 40 cm (4 to 16 inches) long, persist through flowering and die with the plant at the end of the second year. The dead plants often remain upright like brown skeletons.

58

MOUNTAIN DANDELION
Agoseris species
Sunflower family
Compositae

59

Four species of mountain dandelion are known to occur in the park. One, Arizona mountain dandelion (*Agoseris arizonica*), is found on both rims. Two others, shown here, are confined to mountain meadows on the North Rim. The fourth is found at one location in the Inner Gorge.

Orange mountain dandelion (*Agoseris aurantiaca*) has deep orange or brownish-red flowers, an unusual color for flowers in the park. It is found in Kaibab Basin and flowers in August in meadows along the Point Imperial Road.

Its grasslike leaves are all basal, mostly 10 to 15 cm (4 to 6 inches) long. The several flowering stalks are 10 to 60 cm (4 to 24 inches) tall with flowers 25 to 35 mm (1 to 1 1/2 inches) high.

Pale mountain dandelion (*Agoseris glauca*) is very similar to orange mountain dandelion except for its yellow flowers. It grows in many places on the North Rim, including Little Park Lake, at the North Rim entrance station, Robbers Roost, The Basin, and Tiyo Point.

Mountain dandelions, all native species, are different from the common weedy dandelion, which was introduced from Europe.

HAIRY GOLD-ASTER
Heterotheca villosa
Sunflower family
Compositae

A loosely branched, leafy herb with scattered yellow flowers, hairy gold-aster is found on both rims and in the upper parts of the Inner Canyon. It is common in the pinyon-juniper woodland around Grand Canyon Village and along West Rim Drive. On the North Rim it grows at Cape Royal and Greenland Lake.

Hopi Indians made a tea from the leaves and flowers to cure pains in the chest. Navajos planted the seeds with those of squash and melons to ensure a good crop.

Hairy gold-aster stems are usually 10 to 50 cm (4 to 20 inches) tall, and larger plants are somewhat woody and bushy. The flowers, usually about 25 mm (1 inch) across, have yellow rays and centers. Oval or narrower leaves usually less than 25 mm long are numerous on the stems.

60

RAGLEAF, YELLOW RAGWEED
Bahia dissecta
Sunflower family
Compositae

61

Flowering on both rims in late summer, ragleaf is one of many yellow-flowered members of the Sunflower family. It is a biennial or short-lived perennial found at higher elevations in the Inner Canyon, on the South Rim along the East Rim Drive, around Tusayan Ruin, and on the North Rim at the entrance station, Robbers Roost, and Walhalla Plateau.

The stems grow 10 to 80 cm (4 to 32 inches) tall and have sticky glandular hairs in the flowering portion. The branched inflorescence has several flowers with yellow rays (petals) and slightly darker yellow centers. The flowers are about 25 mm (1 inch) across. Deeply cleft leaves, divided two or three times into narrow segments, are mostly basal but extend up the lower portion of the stem.

YELLOW TACKSTEM
Calycoseris parryi
Sunflower family
Compositae

Bright yellow flowers grace this small winter annual which flowers from March to May in the Inner Gorge and on the Tonto Plateau. As with all of the desert annuals, its abundance is variable from year to year depending on winter rainfall. The plants often grow in other shrubs and on open shaley slopes. At times they make displays of brilliant yellow, visible from considerable distances.

The stems grow 5 to 30 cm (2 to 12 inches) tall, and are simple to much-branched and spreading. The flowers are about 25 to 35 mm (1 to 1 3/8 inches) across and consist of overlapping petals of successively shorter lengths toward the center. The lower leaves are deeply divided, and the upper leaves are narrow and undivided.

62

BRITTLEBUSH
Encelia farinosa
Sunflower family
Compositae

63

Brittlebush is a shrub which is nearly confined to the Inner Gorge, and becomes abundant immediately below the Tonto Platform. For a couple of weeks in late April the bushes are covered with showy yellow flowers, and their density is such that the faint yellow color they impart to the cliffs and slopes can be seen from the Canyon rim. The flowers, solitary on long stalks, rise well above the leafy branches of the shrub.

Brittlebush is so named because the stems break very easily. The stems exude a gum that was chewed by the Indians and was also used as incense in the churches of Baja California. The plants are reported to be browsed by bighorn sheep.

The rounded shrubs reach a height of 30 to 100 cm (1 to 3 feet), branching at the base from a short, woody trunk. The flowers are about 25 mm (1 inch) across with yellow petals (rays) and a yellow center. The large grayish-green leaves, clustered at the

ends of the branches, are oval in shape and without teeth. During dry periods the leaves drop and some stems may even die, but following soaking rains the plants quickly revive and resume growth. Brittlebush is a dominant shrub in much of the Sonoran Desert in southern Arizona and northern Mexico and reaches a northeastern limit along the Colorado River in the Grand Canyon.

RAYLESS GUMWEED
Grindelia aphanactis
Sunflower family
Compositae

Flowers lacking obvious petals and a general stickiness are characteristics of rayless gumweed. Blooming from late July through September, it may be seen along roadsides in Grand Canyon Village and along West Rim Drive. Curlycup gumweed (*Grindelia squarrosa*), a closely related plant which is similarly sticky and has yellow petals, is found flowering in summer in the Grandview area and at other South Rim locations.

Some species of gumweed have been used medicinally for kidney disorders, rheumatism, and to cure poison ivy rash. The plants are probably toxic.

Rayless gumweed is an annual or biennial with branched stems 25 to 40 cm (10 to 16 inches) tall. The yellow flowering heads are 10 to 30 mm (3/8 to 1 1/4 inches) wide, the green bracts underneath being very sticky and resinous. The rather narrow leaves, 1 to 6 cm (3/8 to 2 3/8 inches) long, are also resinous and have numerous oily glands on the surface.

64

SPINY GOLDENWEED
Haplopappus spinulosus
Sunflower family
Compositae

65

There are at least thirteen different species of goldenweed in the park growing at all elevations and showing a diversity of growth form. This one is a somewhat shrubby perennial found in the Inner Canyon mostly below the Tonto Plateau. Flowering mainly from late February through May, it can flower again in late summer and early fall if there is still enough moisture on the desert slopes when the summer heat lets up.

The specific name for this plant comes from the presence of bristle-tipped teeth on the leaves. The plant itself is not spiny. The sparingly branched stems are 20 to 60 cm (8 to 24 inches) tall with large yellow flowers having many pointed petals (rays) each 8 to 15 mm (1/4 to 5/8 inch) long.

COMMON SUNFLOWER
Helianthus annuus
Sunflower family
Compositae

SOUTH RIM
Flowers: July-September

Common sunflower, one of our tallest annual species, lends a splash of color to northern Arizona fields and roadsides in late summer. Within the park, it grows along the railroad tracks in the village and along the East Rim Drive. It is more abundant near Flagstaff, where it covers many acres with a sea of yellow flowers. A closely related species, prairie sunflower (*Helianthus petiolaris*), is also found in the park; it is somewhat smaller and is difficult to distinguish from common sunflower.

This widespread plant was cultivated by Indians on the shores of Lake Huron before they were contacted by Europeans. Indians obtained fiber from the stems and a yellow dye from the flowers. The seeds were eaten and used to produce a purple and black dye, and sunflower oil. The cultivated sunflower was developed (in Russia) from this species and is widely planted for its beauty and its large, tasty seeds.

The wild plants grow 30 to 200 cm (1 to 6 1/2 feet) tall and begin to flower in June. The height of flowering occurs after summer rains in August and early September. The large flowers, 50 to 75 mm (2 to 3 inches) across, have wide yellow rays and purple-brown centers. The large, oval leaves are 4 to 20 cm (1 1/2 to 8 inches) long, and are roughly hairy, like sandpaper. The plants develop rapidly with rain and the warm summer sun. They are frost-sensitive, and their flowering comes to an abrupt halt with the first hard frost in the fall.

HYMENOPAPPUS
Hymenopappus filifolius var. *lugens*
Sunflower family
Compositae

67

White woolly stems and leaves, and raggedy, rayless flowering heads distinguish hymenopappus which flowers from May to July on both rims. On the South Rim the plants may be found in Grand Canyon Village, at Desert View, and around Tusayan Ruin. On the North Rim it grows along Cape Royal Road and at Tiyo Point.

The root of hymenopappus is reported to be used by Hopis as an emetic and in treating toothache. Navajos treated wounds with a preparation of the herb.

The perennial plants, with one or several stems from a branching root crown, grow 10 to 50 cm (4 to 20 inches) tall with yellow flowers less than 12 mm (1/2 inch) across. The leaves, mostly located at the base of the plant, are twice divided into narrow segments and are 50 to 90 mm (2 to 3 1/2 inches) long.

GREENSTEM PAPERFLOWER
Psilostrophe sparsiflora
Sunflower family
Compositae

Greenstem paperflower is easily distinguished from the many other yellow members of the Sunflower family by its few, very wide petals (rays). Nearly as wide as they are long, the rays persist, dried and faded, on the flowers for weeks. Usually flowering from April to August, the plants are especially common in pinyon-juniper woodland on the South Rim, as at Hermits Rest, and in the Inner Canyon woodlands down to the Redwall Limestone.

The stems, often many from one plant, are mostly 15 to 35 cm (6 to 14 inches) tall. The central disk of the flowers is small and the rays are 6 to 12 mm (1/4 to 1/2 inch) in length. Long, narrow, dark green leaves are scattered along the stems.

68

TALL GOLDENROD
Solidago altissima
Sunflower family
Compositae

69

Tall goldenrod is a summer flowering species of sunny meadows and other open places on both rims. Grandview Point is a good place to see it on the South Rim, and it grows in meadows along the Point Imperial Road. There are six species of goldenrod in the park, and some of them are rather difficult to tell apart. One distinctive feature of most goldenrods, including tall goldenrod, is their branched inflorescence with flowers on only one side.

The stems of tall goldenrod, solitary or in clumps, are 60 to 150 cm (2 to 5 feet) tall. The yellow flowering heads are 3 to 5 mm (about 1/8 inch) high, arranged along the upper side of the spreading branches of the inflorescence. The leaves, placed along the entire stem but becoming gradually smaller toward the top, mostly have smooth, non-toothed edges and

are up to 12 cm (4 3/4 inches) long. This somewhat variable species is widely distributed, being found from the Atlantic Coast states, where it is an abundant late-summer wildflower in old fields, to Wyoming and Arizona.

COMMON DANDELION
Taraxacum officinale
Sunflower family
Compositae

No book on wildflowers would be complete without the common dandelion! The familiar yellow-flowered plant is found throughout North America and was introduced from Europe. In the park it is found from the shores of the Colorado River to the high elevation meadows on the North Rim. It is often seen in disturbed areas with some moisture and along roadsides, but it may also show up in forests, springs, and other natural areas.

Dandelions have been widely used for food and medicinal purposes. The leaves are used raw for greens or cooked. The roots may be eaten raw in salads or cooked in stew; they also have medicinal effect and have been used for centuries throughout the world as a tonic, mild laxative, and diuretic. The roasted root has been used as a substitute for coffee, and the flower heads may be used to make wine.

Dandelion leaves are all basal, arising from a long taproot. The flowering stalks grow 5 to 30 cm (2 to 12 inches) tall, with heads 15 to 50 mm (5/8 to 2 inches) across. The heads consist entirely of many tiny ray flowers, without the different central flowers found in many other composites. The universal distribution of the plants is a result of the feather-like parachute on the seeds, allowing them to be easily dispersed over long distances by the wind.

GOATSBEARD, SALSIFY
Tragopogon dubius
Sunflower family
Compositae

71

Introduced from Europe as a food source by early colonists, goatsbeard has spread widely through North America. This species is common on both rims and is rather conspicuous with its tall stems, grasslike leaves, yellow flowers, and especially the large, round, feathery seed heads. Each seed develops a stalk with a fluffy crown which serves to disperse it, much like the common dandelion. The plants are usually seen in flower from June through August.

The salsifies were cultivated for their fleshy taproots, which taste like parsnips when cooked. They were used by the Indians for food after they escaped from cultivation. Indians chewed the coagulated juice for its medicinal value in relieving indigestion.

The stems of goatsbeard are from 30 to 90 cm (12 to 36 inches) tall. The flowering heads are all rays, and underneath the petals are pointed bracts,

alternating with and longer than the rays. The narrow leaves are 3 to 25 cm (1 1/4 to 10 inches) long, usually clasping the stem at the base and arching downward at the tip.

Grand Canyon June 1995

With its abundance of bright yellow flowers, trixis is an attractive shrub flowering in late winter and spring in the Inner Canyon, mainly from the Tonto Plateau to the Colorado River. The flower heads consist entirely of tiny flowers each with two curled strap-like petals. There are only a few members of the Sunflower family which have two petals per flower, and trixis is the only one in the park which is yellow. The plants begin flowering in February in the Inner Gorge. While not as numerous as other shrubs such as brittlebush, they are not hard to find on the steep, rocky slopes.

The profusely branched shrubs grow up to 1 m (3 1/4 feet) tall with many heads each about 15 mm (5/8 inch) high and containing 9 to 14 flowers. The bright green leaves are nearly evergreen and are 2 to 5 cm (3/4 to 2 inches) long. The edges are often turned under slightly. The Grand Canyon is the northern limit of trixis; it is found in desert areas from western Texas to southern California.

SHOWY GOLDENEYE
Viguiera multiflora
Sunflower family
Compositae

73

Open, rocky meadows in the pine forest are good places to find showy goldeneye, a late summer flowering plant which often provides displays if summer rains have been plentiful. Although the plants start flowering as early as May, their main season is in August and September, and they are among the last of the meadow plants still in full flower when frost season rolls around.

The plants are perennial herbs, dying back each winter. Loosely branched upright stems 25 to 100 cm (10 to 39 inches) tall have numerous yellow flowers about 5 cm (2 inches) in diameter near the ends of the branches. The heads have eight to twelve yellow, pointed rays and yellow, sometimes darker, centers. The narrow leaves are usually paired at least in the lower part of the plant.

Claretcup hedgehog and Indian paintbrush

LITTLELEAF MOUNTAIN-MAHOGANY
Cercocarpus ledifolius var. *intricatus*

Rose family
Rosaceae

75

While its flowers are very small, littleleaf mountain-mahogany is a conspicuous shrub along the rims where it does well growing from cracks in the exposed bedrock. As the scientific name suggests, it is an intricately branched shrub, with stiff, even spinescent branches. Its small, leathery leaves are the most noticeable feature: they are very narrow and the edges are strongly inrolled, nearly obscuring the underside. The viewpoints along the East Rim Drive are good places to see littleleaf mountain-mahogany.

A beautiful red dye may be obtained from the bark and roots of this shrub. It provides excellent browse for deer, bighorn sheep, and domestic livestock.

The plants are 30 to 150 cm (1 to 5 feet) tall, and the evergreen leaves are 5 to 15 mm (1/4 to 5/8 inch) in length. After flowering the styles elongate, forming feathery tails 20 to 50 mm (3/4 to 2 inches) long.

OLDMAN-WHISKERS
Geum triflorum
Rose family
Rosaceae

With its unusual nodding flowers and whiskery fruits, oldman-whiskers is one of the first flowers to appear in spring on the Canyon rims. The showy red sepals nearly hide the small pinkish or whitish petals, and after flowering the styles elongate into long gray tails protruding from the flowers, giving the plant its name. Usually found in ponderosa pine forests, the plants turn green and flower soon after the snow melts in early spring. Flowering may persist into June in some places.

A perennial with a thick underground stem, oldman-whiskers has fern-like leaves at the base of the plant and a nearly leafless flowering stalk 20 to 50 cm (8 to 20 inches) tall. The plume-like styles protrude 2 to 4 cm (3/4 to 1 1/2 inches) from the downturned flowers.

GLOBEMALLOW
Sphaeralcea grossulariaefolia
Mallow family
Malvaceae

77

Nine species of globemallow have been reported from the Grand Canyon, most of which are rather difficult to distinguish. The flowers of all of them are quite similar, and the leaves are variable within each of the species. This species is commonly found from just below the rim to the Inner Gorge; it is especially common at the lower edge of the woodland and on the Tonto Platform. On the rims and along the Colorado River it is replaced by one or more other species.

There are few places in the Canyon below the spruce-fir forest where one cannot find globemallows. When moisture is available they flower most of the year in the Inner Gorge; on the rims the flowering season is from May to October.

The plants have been used by Hopis for various medicinal purposes and the stems were chewed as a substitute for chewing gum. They are also browsed to some extent by bighorn sheep.

The plants are much branched from the base giving them a shrubby appearance, and grow 70 to 100 cm (32 to 40 inches) tall. The overlapping orange petals form a bowl-shaped flower about 2.5 cm (1 inch) across. The herbage is somewhat grayish due to a dense covering of minute, star-shaped hairs.

Grand Canyon June 1995

CLARETCUP HEDGEHOG
Echinocereus triglochidiatus

SOUTH RIM
NORTH RIM
INNER CANYON
Flowers: April-June

Cactus family
Cactaceae

Of the two hedgehog cacti in the park, claretcup is the most widespread. It is often seen with its many bright red flowers opening in May and June on the rims, and in late April in the Inner Canyon. Yavapai Point and the Grandview to Desert View areas are good places to see it on the South Rim, and it is found at Cape Royal on the North Rim. Although it is found along the Colorado River in places, the Engelmann hedgehog replaces it as the more abundant species in the Inner Gorge.

Except in very young plants, claretcup grows in clumps of a few to many stems; large plants have several hundred and may be a meter or more in diameter. The stems grow about 7 to 15 cm (3 to 6 inches) tall with numerous spines 2.5 to 5 cm (1 to 2 inches) long. The beautiful red flowers are about 3 cm (1 1/4 inches) in diameter and about 2 to 3 cm (1 inch) long. The red petals are offset by the green stigmas in the center of the flower.

Grand Canyon June 1995

PINEDROPS
Pterospora andromeda
Heath family
Ericaceae

An attractive non-green plant of the pine forests, pinedrops obtains its food from decaying wood or leaf-mold, as it is unable to make its own through photosynthesis. The reddish flowering stalks appear from June through August and may be seen on both rims.

Usually appearing in clusters of several stems, the plants grow 20 to 100 cm (8 to 40 inches) tall. The leaves are small and scale-like against the stems. Nodding flowers appear in large numbers over the upper two-thirds or three-quarters of the stems. The plants are very glandular and feel sticky-clammy to the touch.

BUTTERFLYWEED
Asclepias tuberosa
Milkweed family
Asclepiadaceae

With its showy clusters of orange-red flowers, butterfly-weed is the most colorful of the five true milkweeds in the Grand Canyon. It is uncommon in the park, found mainly in open places in pine forests on the North Rim where it flowers from June to August. Flower color varies from yellow to dark orange. Unlike most members of the genus, butterflyweed has clear rather than milky sap. The plant is widely distributed in the United States.

Growing about 30 to 80 cm (12 to 32 inches) tall, the leafy stems have several clusters of flowers at the top. Many small flowers are present in each cluster. The typical milkweed pods are 7 to 10 cm (2 3/4 to 4 inches) long.

PAINTBRUSH
Castilleja species

Figwort family
Scrophulariaceae

81

Of five species of paintbrush common in the park, the two most widespread are shown here. Although they overlap considerably in their distribution, wholeleaf paintbrush, *Castilleja integra*, is more common in dry, sunny places in woodlands and forests of the South Rim, while narrow-leaved paintbrush, *Castilleja linariaefolia*, is found scattered on both rims and the Inner Canyon.

Flowering from March through September, wholeleaf paintbrush is conspicuous with its bright red color. As in all paintbrushes, the color is due to red leaflike bracts under each flower. It is a perennial, with several stems 10 to 40 cm (4 to 16 inches) tall, each topped with

a flower cluster 4 to 8 cm (1 1/2 to 3 inches) long. Wholeleaf paintbrush differs from narrow-leaved paintbrush in being somewhat shorter, having broader leaves, and fewer, more rounded, and wider red floral bracts.

Narrow-leaved paintbrush may be seen flowering from April to October, depending on elevation. On the South Rim, look for it growing with sagebrush along East Rim Drive. On the North Rim it often

Grand Canyon June 1995

Wholeleaf paintbrush

Narrow-leaved paintbrush

Narrow-leaved
SOUTH RIM
NORTH RIM
INNER CANYON
TOROWEAP
Flowers: April-October

occurs on the edge of meadows, and in the Inner Canyon it is occasionally found in rocky areas of side canyons. The plants are perennial, with several purplish stems up to 75 cm (30 inches) tall, and the leaves are long and very narrow. Flower clusters are dense and spikelike, with long, bright red bracts narrowly divided into slender lobes.

Paintbrush plants are at least partially parasitic on the roots of other plants. Their roots penetrate tissues of the host plant to obtain some of their food. This is why paintbrushes are usually seen growing among shrubs, and often the bright red flowers are mistaken for those of the host. Hopi people ate the flowers raw and used various parts of the plants medicinally and ceremonially.

SKYROCKET
Ipomopsis aggregata
Phlox family
Polemoniaceae

83

One of the showiest summer wildflowers of Arizona, skyrocket is abundant in places on the North Rim, found in a few places on the South Rim, and is scattered in the upper parts of the Inner Canyon. It is usually found in ponderosa pine forests and open meadows at higher elevations. In certain areas around Flagstaff, fields turn red in late summer with a spectacular display of skyrocket.

Two variants occur on the North Rim: the normal bright red-flowered plants are most common, and in a few places, particularly near the junction of the Cape Royal Road and the North Rim Entrance Road, a pink-flowered form occurs. Both are shown here.

The red flowers are pollinated by hummingbirds seeking nectar. Deer and pronghorn reportedly browse the plants.

The plants are biennial or perennial, flowering the second year. The first year a rosette of finely divided leaves is produced; the second and following years flowering stems 15 to 80 cm (6 to 32 inches) tall develop in late spring. Flowers on the upper half or more of the unbranched stems begin to open in early summer, often after the first summer rains. The petals are united into a tube 20 to 45 mm (3/4 to 1 3/4 inches) long with flaring pointed tips.

Grand Canyon June 1995

CRIMSON MONKEYFLOWER
Mimulus cardinalis

Figwort family
Scrophulariaceae

Crimson monkeyflower is one of the species sure to be present in large shady seeps and along most permanently-running streams in the Inner Canyon. Dripping Springs, Pipe Creek along the Bright Angel Trail, Phantom Ranch, and Ribbon Falls are a few of its localities accessible on foot from the rims. Vasey's Paradise, Elves Chasm, and lower Havasu Canyon, accessible from the river, have large populations of crimson monkeyflower. It is one of seven species of *Mimulus* recorded within the park; one of the other species is a purple-flowered annual living on rocky desert slopes, a habitat at an opposite extreme from the watery domicile of crimson monkeyflower.

The plants grow more or less erect, usually clumped, from 25 to 90 cm (10 to 36 inches) tall with flowers arising at the top on long, slender stalks. The irregular, two-lipped flowers, with petals joined in a long tube, are about 5 cm (2 inches) long. Large, paired leaves, 2 to 8 cm (3/4 to 4 1/4 inches) long, are closely spaced along the stems. The leaves have several obvious parallel veins giving them a furrowed appearance.

84

PENSTEMON, BEARDTONGUE

Penstemon species

Figwort family
Scrophulariaceae

85

The penstemons of Grand Canyon National Park can be divided into two major groupings: pink or purple flowered species mostly with inflated flowers, and red flowered species with elongate flowers. Shown here are three of the most common red flowered species: Utah penstemon, Eaton or firecracker penstemon, and scarlet bugler.

Utah penstemon (*Penstemon utahensis*) is a beautiful plant, sending forth long wands of scarlet flowers in April and May at higher elevations in the Inner Canyon from the rim to the Supai Formation. It may be seen along the Kaibab, Bright Angel, and Hermit Trails. Its distinctive characteristic is the five broadly spreading rounded lobes of the petals at the outer end of the floral tube. The plants grow 15 to 70 cm (6 to 28 inches) tall with several large basal leaves and small, narrower leaves arranged in pairs along the stems.

Of the three, Eaton penstemon (*Penstemon eatoni*) has the widest geographical range in the Canyon, occurring both on the rims and scattered in the Inner Gorge. It flowers in early April in dry side canyons near the Colorado River, in April and May along the Inner Canyon trails (sometimes growing with Utah penstemon) and at Yavapai Point and Point Sublime on the rims in June and July. It differs from Utah penstemon in that it

Utah

Eaton

Eaton
SOUTH RIM
NORTH RIM
INNER CANYON
TOROWEAP
Flowers: April-July

Scarlet bugler
SOUTH RIM
NORTH RIM
Flowers: June-October

lacks the flared lobes at the end of the tube. In contrast, the small lobes often nearly close the opening. The plants grow 30 to 100 cm (12 to 39 inches) tall, and the leaves are somewhat wider than those of the other species and are paired on the stem. Flowers are present on the upper half of the stem.

Apparently not found below the rims, scarlet bugler (*Penstemon barbatus*) has the highest elevational distribution of the three red penstemons. It flowers later in the season than the others, from June through October. On the North Rim it is very common along the Point Sublime Road in deep forests, at Greenland Spring, and at the entrance station. On the South Rim it is found at Desert View and along the East and West Rim Drives. Its flowers are intermediate between the other two, with an upper straight tip and lower lip that is turned back.

The plants are 40 to 140 cm (16 to 55 inches) tall with an elongate, loosely flowered inflorescence. Leaves are similar to those of the other two species.

The red-flowered penstemons are mostly pollinated by hummingbirds whose needlelike bills are capable of reaching the nectar located at the base of the floral tube.

Scarlet bugler

ARIZONA THISTLE
Cirsium arizonicum
Sunflower family
Compositae

87

The ten species of thistle in Grand Canyon National Park range in color from white to purple to red. Arizona thistle is one of two red species; they are similar in appearance and difficult to distinguish. Flowering from May to October, Arizona thistle is found scattered on the South Rim and for a short distance below. The plants are well armed, with long spines on the leaves, stems, and bracts of the flower heads.

Arizona thistle is a stout plant, branched in the upper part and growing 60 cm (24 inches) tall or more. The heads, 3 to 4 cm (1 1/4 to 1 5/8 inches) high, consist of many tiny bright red disk flowers, all upright and appearing like a small red brush. The leaves are deeply divided and are very spiny.

Grand Canyon June 1995

Grassleaf peavine

89

"When your spirit cries for peace, come to a land of canyons deep in an old land; feel the exultation of high plateaus, the strength of moving waters, the simplicity of sand and grass, and silence of growth."

- August Fruge

WEAKSTEM MARIPOSA LILY
Calochortus flexuosus
Lily family
Liliaceae

90

Although it is a perennial, growing from a bulb that may be as much as 15 cm (6 inches) underground, the flowering of this Inner Canyon lily is strongly dependent upon the amount of winter rainfall. In April following wet winters, they make beautiful displays of light pink or lavender flowers along the Plateau Point and Clear Creek Trails and many other areas on the Tonto Plateau. After dry winters few plants produce flowers, many having only a single narrow leaf and others remaining completely dormant. The edible bulbs were used by Navajos and Hopis.

The flowering stems are 15 to 40 cm (6 to 16 inches) long and are often somewhat twisted like short vines. Several flowers usually appear at intervals along the stem. The three oval petals are 3 to 4 cm (1 1/4 to 1 1/2 inches) long, varying in color from nearly white to light pink or pale purple.

TRAILING FOUR-O'CLOCK, WINDMILLS

Allionia incarnata

Four-o'clock family

Nyctaginaceae

91

Trailing four-o'clock is a denizen of the Inner Gorge, flowering from spring through summer and into fall from the Tonto Plateau to the Colorado River. The showy rose-purple flowers open at dawn and stay open for only a few hours, wilting by noon in the midday desert heat. The plants may be seen at Indian Gardens, Plateau Point, Phantom Ranch, Ribbon Falls, and Havasu Canyon, flowering in April and May and, if summer rains are sufficient, flowering more profusely from late July through September. The common name "windmills" is sometimes applied to the plant because under favorable conditions long trailing stems, sometimes 2 or 3 m (6 to 10 feet) long, radiate spokelike from the center of the plant and are blown like a windmill by summer desert breezes.

Large plants make colorful displays with many flowers opening at once. The flowers, about 2 cm (3/4 inch) across, actually consist of three individual irregular flowers arranged to look like a single blossom. Trailing four-o'clock is a conspicuous late-summer desert and roadside wildflower from Arizona into western Texas. It is also found in the deserts of Central and South America.

Grand Conyon June 1995

COLORADO FOUR-O'CLOCK

Mirabilis multiflora
Four-o'clock family
Nyctaginaceae

With its dense foliage of dark green leaves and brilliant magenta flowers, Colorado four-o'clock is one of the showiest plants on the Colorado Plateau. Flowering in spring and again after summer rains, it is frequently encountered along roadsides on the rims, especially near Desert View, and in rocky areas along trails in the Inner Canyon. The flowers open in late afternoon, remain open through the night, and wither shortly after daybreak.

The flowers arise in clusters of 8 to 12, with one or two in a cluster opening each day. Each flower is about 2 to 3 cm (1 inch) across and 5 cm (2 inches) long. The cultivated four-o'clock is closely related, similar in appearance, and is a native of South America.

92

PERENNIAL ROCKCRESS
Arabis perennans
Mustard family
Cruciferae

93

One of the earliest blooming spring wildflowers in the Grand Canyon is perennial rockcress. It may be found blossoming in the Inner Gorge in February and has a progressively later flowering season at higher elevations. It appears on the South Rim in April and on the North Rim in June. It is common in the woodlands of the rims, and grows from cracks in rock walls in the Inner Canyon. Although rather inconspicuous, the purple four-petaled flowers are attractive and the plants are sufficiently widespread that they are frequently encountered. Six species of rockcress are found in the park, all having similar flowers. Perennial rockcress is the most common.

The plants are branched at the base with several stems 15 to 30 cm (6 to 12 inches) tall. Most of the leaves are in a rosette at the base of the plant; a few smaller leaves occur on the stem. The flowers, each about 1 cm (3/8 inch) in diameter, are in an open arrangement along the upper half of the stem.

PURPLE BLADDERPOD
Lesquerella purpurea

Mustard family
Cruciferae

There are six species of bladderpod in the Grand Canyon, five of which have yellow flowers. The white or purple flowers of this species are unusual, but the small spherical pods are distinctive and typical of the genus. Purple bladderpod is commonly encountered in April and May in the Inner Canyon, particularly below the Tonto Plateau on ledges along the Kaibab, Bright Angel, and Hermit Trails. It is often seen growing near perennial rockcress, which differs in having elongate slender pods.

The only annual species of bladderpod in Arizona, *Lesquerella gordoni,* covers extensive areas in the desert with its yellow flowers. Its most colorful displays are usually seen in broad valleys rather than in topographically complex areas like the Grand Canyon.

Purple bladderpod stems are usually 10 to 50 cm (4 to 20 inches) tall, with most of the leaves at the base. The flowers are rather dense at the end of the stems, which elongate in fruit. The flowers are about 10 mm (3/8 inch) in diameter, and are white streaked with purple, fading to purple all over.

94

ROCKY MOUNTAIN BEEPLANT
Cleome serrulata
Cleome family
Cleomaceae

SOUTH RIM
NORTH RIM
Flowers: June-September

95

A tall, attractive annual, Rocky Mountain beeplant flowers in late summer along roadsides and in disturbed areas. It grows in a few places in Grand Canyon Village, especially near the old railroad station and along the tracks. It is more common along the highways which approach the park from the south than within the park itself. Since it is an annual, responding to summer rains, its abundance depends on the amount of moisture brought in by summer thundershowers.

As the common name indicates, beeplants are considered a good source for honey. The seeds are eaten by doves. Hopis and Navajos are reported to have used the young plants as potherbs. Two other species of beeplant occur in northern Arizona, both with yellow flowers. These have been collected at lower elevations in the park, at Toroweap Point, and along the Colorado River in Marble Canyon.

Rocky Mountain beeplant grows to a height of 50 to 100 cm (20 to 40 inches), with as much as 25 cm (10 inches) of the upper part of the stems bearing flowers. Like the closely related mustards, beeplant flowers have four long, narrow petals. The showiness of the flowers results from the long purple stamens as well as the petals.

WAX CURRANT
Ribes cereum

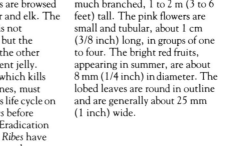

SOUTH RIM
NORTH RIM
INNER CANYON
Flowers: April-July

Saxifrage family
Saxifragaceae

There are seven species of currants and gooseberries known to occur in the Grand Canyon. Two or more species sometimes grow together, and they are often hard to tell apart. Wax currant differs from the others in its lack of spines on the twigs and its white or pink flowers.

Flowering from April to July depending on elevation, wax currant can be seen along the Bright Angel, Hermit and Kaibab Trails, in the woodlands around Grand Canyon Village, along the East Rim Drive, and near the Canyon on the North Rim.

Birds and rodents utilize the fruit, and the shrubs are browsed occasionally by deer and elk. The fruit of this species is not especially palatable but the currants of some of the other species make excellent jelly. Blister rust fungus, which kills 5-needle (white) pines, must spend one stage of its life cycle on some species of *Ribes* before spreading to pines. Eradication programs to destroy *Ribes* have been carried out where there are commercially valuable stands of white pine.

The shrubs are erect and much branched, 1 to 2 m (3 to 6 feet) tall. The pink flowers are small and tubular, about 1 cm (3/8 inch) long, in groups of one to four. The bright red fruits, appearing in summer, are about 8 mm (1/4 inch) in diameter. The lobed leaves are round in outline and are generally about 25 mm (1 inch) wide.

96

SPECKLEPOD LOCOWEED
Astragalus lentiginosus
Pea family
Leguminosae

97

This is the largest genus of flowering plants in Arizona, and, with 21 species, one of the largest in the park. The species are difficult to distinguish and there is considerable variability within some of them. Specklepod locoweed is probably the most common and most widely distributed of the species in the park. One or more of its varieties is found from the rims to the river, flowering on sandy beaches in February and March in the Inner Canyon, on the Hermit and Kaibab Trails in April and May, and at springs on the North Rim in July and August.

Some of the species of *Astragalus* are poisonous to livestock and are known as locoweeds. Once animals start eating the plant they develop an addiction which eventually leads to death from "loco disease." Other species, called poison-vetch, are toxic because they concentrate selenium from the soil. The non-poisonous species are known as milkvetches.

Specklepod loco is a biennial or perennial with numerous stems. Length of the stems, size of the leaves, and number of flowers vary greatly in different varieties of the species. The flowers vary from pink to purple, are 7 to 25 mm (1/4 to 1 inch) long, and are clustered at the ends of the stems. The pods are variably inflated. The leaves are always compound with 11 to 27 leaflets. Stems usually spread along the ground although some, especially those stems or parts of stems with flowers, are upright.

WESTERN REDBUD
Cercis occidentalis
Pea family
Leguminosae

Flowering in early spring before it leafs out, redbud is one of the most colorful of the shrubs and small trees of the Inner Canyon. The twigs, and even the larger branches and the trunk, are covered with numerous showy red-purple flowers, some of which remain after the leaves begin to unfold. The Bright Angel Trail, along the creek below Indian Gardens, is a good place to see redbud blooming in April. It is also common at the old upper floodline of the Colorado River in the upstream portion of the Grand Canyon, and in seeps and moist side canyons, such as Elves Chasm, in the lower part.

Western redbud is closely related to the larger redbud of the eastern United States, a showy small tree in the understory of the deciduous forest where it flowers in spring before the taller trees have leafed out. Along with two other species of redbud from southern Europe and Asia, it is often planted as an ornamental. Some California Indians used the strong pliable bark of western redbud for weaving baskets.

Navajos roasted the pods, ate the seeds, and made an incense from the leaves.

Reaching a maximum height of about 3.5 m (12 feet), redbud is a distinctive plant with its many pealike flowers 8 to 12 mm (1/4 to 1/2 inch) long and its large, rounded leaves 3 to 9 cm (1 1/4 to 3 1/2 inches) across.

The flowers appear in early to mid April, followed by the leaves in late April. By mid May the long flat pods are well formed, turning brown in late summer and often persisting through winter.

GRASSLEAF PEAVINE
Lathyrus graminifolius
Pea family
Leguminosae

99

Grassleaf peavine and several closely related species of peavine and vetch *(Vicia)* are often seen on the woodland and forest floors in the summer. Vinelike and often climbing over other vegetation, rocks, and logs, they have compound leaves. With the largest, most numerous flowers in the group, grassleaf peavine can be quite showy. It extends into the Inner Canyon; the photograph was taken where Bright Angel Trail crosses the rocky wash just above Indian Gardens. Flower color ranges from pink to purple or bluish, and the plants bloom in April at lower elevations and in summer on the South Rim.

The cultivated sweet pea, a native of Sicily, is a member of this genus. Vetches are considered excellent forage crops; peavines are apparently somewhat less palatable.

The irregular peavine flowers, with the upper petal (banner) broad and flaring, are 10 to 15 mm (3/8 to 5/8 inch) long, and occur in clusters of several flowers on the upper parts of the stems. Each leaf has 4 to 12 narrow leaflets ending in a tendril, which is usually prehensile.

ROCKY MOUNTAIN LOCOWEED, PURPLE LOCO

Oxytropis lambertii

SOUTH RIM
NORTH RIM
Flowers: June-September

Pea family
Leguminosae

Like several species of the closely related genus *Astragalus*, also known as locoweeds, Rocky Mountain locoweed is very poisonous to animals. The plants, found in the meadows on the rims, are rather attractive with their several spikes of purple or more often pink flowers. They are more common south of the park on the road to Flagstaff, where they provide colorful roadside displays in late summer.

Poisonous alkaloids, and selenium if present in the soil, account for the harmful effects of locoweeds. They are usually not eaten if better forage is available, but once taken they may become addictive, especially to horses, to the point of being fatal. Rocky Mountain locoweed is one of the most dangerous because it is often found where grass is scarce and it is readily eaten by animals.

The leaves of this species are all basal and are surpassed by the upright, loosely-flowered inflorescences. The flowers are about 12 to 25 mm (1/2 to 1 inch) long. The 7 to 17 leaflets of each leaf are covered with short silvery hairs.

NEW MEXICAN LOCUST
Robinia neomexicana

Pea family
Leguminosae

101

A large shrub or small tree, New Mexican locust is very handsome when flowering. Large clusters of pink flowers appear in early summer, making it perhaps the showiest tree on the North Rim where it is common along the Point Imperial and Entrance roads and near Point Sublime. At lower elevations, it is found only in protected canyon situations.

The flowers are relished by cattle, and mule deer, sheep, and goats browse the plants. Quail and squirrels eat the seeds. However, the bark, roots, and seeds are reported to be poisonous to humans. New Mexico Indians ate the flowers raw, and Hopis used the plant as an emetic and as a treatment for rheumatism. The plants form thickets, freely sprouting from roots, making them valuable for erosion control. Larger stems are sometimes used to make fence posts.

Reaching a height of 7.5 m (25 feet), New Mexican locust is sometimes cultivated as an ornamental for its showy flowers. The drooping flower clusters are 5 to 10 cm (2 to 4 inches) long with many pea-like flowers. The leaves have 9 to 19 rounded leaflets with a pair of thorns at the base, persisting on the twig after the leaves fall.

FILAREE, HERONSBILL, STORKSBILL

Erodium cicutarium

Geranium family
Geraniaceae

102

A native of the Mediterranean region, filaree is believed to have been introduced into the Southwest at an early date by the Spaniards. It is widely distributed in the Grand Canyon, flowering from June to August on the rims, where it is common along roadsides and in disturbed soil, and from February to April in the Inner Canyon, where it is found beside trails and at Phantom Ranch. It is often extremely abundant in early spring along roadsides in desert areas of Arizona. The prostrate plants are round in outline with finely divided leaves radiating from the center.

Filaree is an excellent spring forage plant for livestock and is especially important because of its great abundance. The young plants may be used in salad or cooked as potherbs.

On young plants and in dry periods the flowers arise from the center of the plant on very short stems. After abundant winter rain however, the plants become large and stems bearing many flowers grow 10 to 40 cm (4 to 16 inches) long. The small rose-lavender flowers develop into fruits with a stiff awl-shaped projection. At maturity this column separates with each of the five seeds retaining part of it as a corkscrewlike tail. The tails uncoil when moist and curl when dry, and alternation of wet and dry weather allows the tails to drill the sharp pointed seeds auger-like into the soil. Several species of grass also have the ability to plant themselves in this manner.

PURPLE CRANESBILL, PURPLE GERANIUM
Geranium caespitosum

Geranium family
Geraniaceae

103

A common sight in the pine forests of both rims, purple cranesbill flowers most of the summer after the rainy season begins. The attractive perennial gets the name cranesbill from the elongate column formed in the center of the old flower when the plants are in fruit. A closely related species, white cranesbill, replaces it at higher elevations on the North Rim. The cultivated windowbox "geraniums" are actually in a different genus (*Pelargonium*) in the same family.

The more or less erect branched stems are 10 to 90 cm (4 to 36 inches) tall. The flowers have five purple petals and are about 2.5 cm (1 inch) across. With five deeply cut lobes, the leaves are 2 to 4 cm (3/4 to 1 1/2 inches) wide.

ARIZONA BEEHIVE, CORYPHANTHA

Coryphantha vivipara

Cactus family
Cactaceae

A woodland cactus found on both rims, Arizona beehive may go unnoticed until its showy pink flowers appear in June and July. The plants grow in clusters of several short spherical stems, each stem often producing two or three flowers. The plants are nowhere very abundant; they may be encountered in the pinyon-juniper woodland, often in small openings with rocky soil.

Coryphantha is closely related to the fishhook or pincushion *(Mammillaria)*, of which there are two species in the Inner Canyon.

The individual stems are 60 to 80 mm (2 1/2 to 3 1/4 inches) in diameter and as much as twice as high, with numerous straight spines. The flowers are 35 to 60 mm (1 1/4 to 2 1/2 inches) across.

104

Grand Canyon June 1995

ENGELMANN HEDGEHOG
Echinocereus engelmannii
Cactus family
Cactaceae

105

The common hedgehog from the Tonto Platform into the Inner Gorge, Engelmann hedgehog generally has fewer, larger stems than the closely related claretcup cactus, with purplish to magenta rather than red flowers. This species is very abundant growing on the Precambrian schist of the Inner Gorge and can be seen flowering in April and May along any of the trails in the vicinity of Phantom Ranch. The color of the flowers is similar to that of beavertail cactus and grizzly-bear cactus, with which it often grows.

The stems of Engelmann hedgehog are usually clumped in crowded groups of three to six. The stems are taller and the spines longer than those of claretcup. Several flowers about 5 cm (2 inches) in diameter appear on each stem. The numerous petals are more pointed than those of claretcup. Both species have similar green stigmas in the middle of the flower surrounded by a multitude of yellow stamens.

GrandCanyon 1995

BEAVERTAIL CACTUS
Opuntia basilaris
Cactus family
Cactaceae

Spineless joints characterize the beavertail cactus and set it apart from all of our other cacti. The uninitiated who assume that the lack of obvious spines makes the beavertail safe to touch are in for a cruel surprise. In place of spines are hundreds of minute needle-like glochids in each of the areoles on the pads. These are readily detached upon contact with the plant and require forceps to remove them from the fingers or legs of those unlucky enough to acquire them.

Beavertail is an abundant member of the Mohave Desert plant community of the Inner Gorge from Marble Canyon throughout the Grand Canyon below the Muav Limestone. Its colorful magenta flowers appear in April and May, sometimes in large numbers on big plants. Packrats and other rodents eat the fruits and seeds.

Ashy blue-green in color, the pads are usually obovate (larger at the top) in shape and reminiscent of a beaver's tail. The clumps grow 15 to 30 cm (6 to 12 inches) high and 30 to 180 cm (1 to 6 feet) in diameter. The flowers are 5 to 8 cm (2 to 3 inches) in diameter with numerous red stamens with yellow pollen. Although occasionally growing as high as 2500 m (8000 feet), beavertail is most common in the hottest and driest parts of the Mohave and Sonoran Deserts.

GRIZZLY-BEAR CACTUS, MOHAVE PRICKLY-PEAR

Opuntia erinacea

Cactus family

Cactaceae

107

A prickly-pear with unusually long spines, grizzly-bear cactus is found from the rims to the river and is most common on the Tonto Plateau. Its dark pink flowers appear in April and May in the Inner Canyon and in June on the rims. The plant grows in large clumps, with the horizontal stems extending outward and rooting where the pads touch the ground.

The distinctive feature of grizzly-bear cactus is its spine length, up to 10 cm (4 inches) in one variety. The whitish spines are dense on the joints and the longest ones are often twisted. The joints are about 9 cm (3 1/2 inches) long and about 6 cm (2 1/2 inches) wide. Spine length and joint size are quite variable, and hybridization with other species is often a complicating factor in identifying this and other prickly pears. Flower color ranges from pink to rose and may occasionally be yellow.

FIREWEED
Epilobium angustifolium
Evening-primrose family
Onagraceae

NORTH RIM
Flowers: July-September

Fireweed is a very attractive summer wildflower with its showy rose to lilac colored flowers in terminal, spike-like clusters. It is common flowering from July to September along roadsides on the North Rim, especially on the North Rim Entrance Road, and in some of the meadow areas such as The Basin. Widely distributed in the Northern Hemisphere, the common name is derived from its ability to enter burned over areas in an early successional stage.

The seeds have a long tuft of silky hairs which allows them to be distributed over long distances by the wind.

The young shoots and leaves may be boiled as a potherb, or mixed with other raw greens to make a salad. The pith of the stems is good in soup. It is a valuable range forage plant, eaten by deer and elk as well as domestic livestock.

Although the stems can grow up to 2.5 m (7 1/2 feet) tall, the plants at the Grand Canyon rarely exceed 1.5 m (5 feet). They are generally branched only at the base. The four-petaled flowers are about 2.5 cm (1 inch) across. The capsules at maturity are 5 to 8 cm (2 to 3 inches) long.

CLIMBING MILKWEED
Sarcostemma cynanchoides

Milkweed family
Asclepiadaceae

109

One of the few vines in the Inner Canyon, climbing milkweed often forms entangled clumps of considerable size on rocks, cliffs, and other vegetation. The North Kaibab Trail along Bright Angel Creek, a short distance above Phantom Ranch, is a good place to find large plants. Climbing milkweed prefers rocky side canyons or rugged slopes in the Inner Gorge. Clusters of many white and purple flowers are seen on the plants from April to July. The sap is milky, like that of most other milkweeds, and has a disagreeable musky odor if the plants are crushed or the stems broken.

Indians are reported to have eaten the fruits raw or cooked.

The stems of climbing milkweed are up to 2 m (6 feet) long, often forming intricate mats. The flowers, are about 10 mm (3/8 inch) across. The pods are about 3 to 11 cm (1 1/4 to 4 1/4 inches) long and contain many seeds each with a tuft of hair allowing airborne distribution. The flowers and pods are very much like those of the more familiar milkweeds; the vinelike habit sets climbing milkweed apart.

DESERT PHLOX
Phlox austromontana
Phlox family
Polemoniaceae

Dense cushions or mats of desert phlox put forth a mass of brilliant pink and white flowers in spring. The gradation in color from deep pink to pure white is a striking feature, and large clumps show every imaginable intermediate shade. Flowering in April in the Inner Canyon, it is commonly seen along the Hermit, Bright Angel and Kaibab Trails. Desert phlox is also abundant on the rims flowering in May and June. The three species of phlox found in the park have similarly colored flowers, but the species differ in the shape of the petals, and in the general habit of the plants.

The low plants of desert phlox have much-branched, short, woody stems giving them a dense clustered appearance. The showy flowers, 10 to 15 mm (3/8 to 5/8 inch) across, appear in large numbers nearly obscuring the plant. Needle-like stiff leaves 10 to 15 mm (3/8 to 5/8 inch) long are a distinctive feature of this species of phlox.

110

LONGLEAF PHLOX
Phlox longifolia
Phlox family
Polemoniaceae

111

Perhaps more common on the rims than desert phlox, longleaf phlox is a taller species with longer, more supple leaves, taller stems and longer, narrower petals. It is common in the pinyon-juniper woodland on the South Rim, flowering during May and June in Grand Canyon Village, along the East Rim Drive, and in the Canyon along the Hermit and Bright Angel Trails a short distance below the rims. Flower color varies from rose to white.

Longleaf phlox is a branched perennial with stems 6 to 30 cm (2 1/2 to 12 inches) tall. Its flowers are 15 to 20 mm (5/8 to 3/4 inch) across and the leaves are 2 to 8 cm (3/4 to 3 inches) long.

TALL VERBENA
Verbena macdougalii
Verbena family
Verbenaceae

112

Tall verbena is a conspicuous summer-flowering plant on both rims. It may be seen around Grand Canyon Village near the Visitor Center, near Rowes Well, and on the East Rim Drive, flowering from June to September. With its small dense purple flowering heads it is rather distinctive; its general appearance is mint-like.

Preparations of the plant are reported to have been used by Navajos for treating fevers and for ceremonial purposes.

Growing 30 to 80 cm (12 to 32 inches) tall, the plants are usually clumped with several erect stems branched at the top into several flowering spikes. The flowers open first at the bottom of the stalk and appear sequentially up the stem, giving the appearance of a purple ring moving slowly upward. The undivided leaves are 2.5 to 7.5 cm (1 to 3 inches) long, coarsely toothed, and prominently veined.

DAKOTA VERVAIN
Glandularia bipinnatifida
Verbena family
Verbenaceae

113

In contrast to the narrow spike-like inflorescence of tall verbena *(Verbena macdougalii),* Dakota vervain has a broad, flat-topped cluster of flowers. The habit of the plants is also different, this species being much-branched at the base rather than tall and upright. Flowering in summer, Dakota vervain may be seen at the junction of the East Rim Drive and the South Entrance Road near Grand Canyon Village. Another species with similar flowers, Gooddings verbena, flowers in the spring in the Inner Canyon.

The plants grow 10 to 60 cm (4 to 24 inches) tall and the blue or purple flowers are each 6 to 8 mm (1/4 to 3/8 inch) wide.

FIELD MINT
Mentha arvensis
Mint family
Labiatae

A strong mint aroma and the unusual arrangement of the flowers characterize field mint, a perennial herb found mainly on the North Rim. Flowering in July and August, it is usually found in deep woods and in moist, shady canyons. The pink to purple flowers occur in dense clusters at intervals along the stem, giving the inflorescence an interrupted appearance.

Peppermint and spearmint are two closely related Old World species commonly cultivated for use in flavoring and for medicinal purposes. Hopis used mint leaves of the native species for flavoring mush. The leaves, lightly steeped in hot water, make delicious beverages. They can also be used to make jelly.

The stems are 10 to 80 cm (4 to 32 inches) tall, usually branched and often clumped from spreading underground stems. The leaves are lance-shaped to oval, 2 to 5 cm (3/4 to 2 inches) long. Field mint is circumpolar in distribution and is found throughout most of North America.

TWINING SNAPDRAGON
Maurandya antirrhiniflora

Figwort family
Scrophulariaceae

115

An attractive plant with pink or purple snapdragon-like flowers and climbing stems, twining snapdragon is an Inner Gorge species, flowering mostly from March through May. It is often seen growing from crevices on the walls of shady side canyons as along Pipe Creek on the Bright Angel Trail and just above Phantom Ranch on the North Kaibab Trail. It is not a true snapdragon, although it is fairly closely related.

Twining snapdragon, as the name suggests, is a viny plant climbing freely over rocks, cliffs, and other vegetation, often growing 2 m (6 1/2 feet) long. The flowers, arising individually in the axils of the leaves but often densely covering portions of the plant, are each 25 to 30 mm (1 to 1 1/4 inch) long with the petals fused and flared outward at the opening. The leaves are triangular and sharply pointed, varying from 5 to 25 mm (1/4 to 1 inch) long.

PURPLE-WHITE OWL-CLOVER
Orthocarpus purpureo-albus

Figwort family
Scrophulariaceae

Similar in appearance to the paintbrushes (*Castilleja* species) but differing in flower color and the fact that it is an annual instead of a perennial, purple-white owl-clover grows in sunny, dry meadows mainly on the North Rim. The handsome purple and white flowers appear from July to September in open upright clusters on slender unbranched or few-branched stems. A closely related species, yellow owl clover, has yellow flowers and often grows with this species.

Purple-white owl clover grows 10 to 40 cm (4 to 16 inches) tall with terminal flowering spikes 2 to 15 cm (3/4 to 6 inches) long. The flowers are about 12 to 20 mm (1/2 to 3/4 inch) long. Its leaves are divided into three very narrow lobes.

WOOD-BETONY, LOUSEWORT
Pedicularis centranthera
Figwort family
Scrophulariaceae

One of the early spring flowers on the rims, wood-betony appears on the South Rim along the South Rim Trail, near the Visitor Center, and in the Grandview area in April. On the North Rim it appears near the entrance station and along the Transept Trail in June. It is quite common, often flowering shortly after the snow melts in both pinyon-juniper woodland and ponderosa pine forest. The plants are partly root-parasitic.

Distinctive features of wood-betony include purplish-green leaves which have doubly toothed lobes partway to the midrib, and leafless stalks with clusters of peculiarly-shaped flowers which are whitish at the base with purple tips.

The flowering stems are about 3 to 15 cm (1 1/4 to 6 inches) tall with relatively few but densely arranged flowers 30 to 35 mm (1 1/4 to 1 3/8 inches) long. The fern-like leaves are 5 to 15 cm (2 to 6 inches) long, arising in a rosette at the base of the plant.

BROOMRAPE
Orobanche fasciculata

Broomrape family
Orobanchaceae

Completely lacking chlorophyll, broomrape is non-photosynthetic and parasitic, relying wholly on other plants for food, water, and nutrients. Frequently the hosts are big sagebrush or wild buckwheat. The somewhat fleshy clumped stems with small, scalelike leaves produce purplish flowers with yellow centers on long, erect stalks. Flowering from May to July, the plant may be seen near the Visitor Center on the South Rim Trail, on the West Rim Trail, at Yavapai Point on the South Rim, and at Cape Royal and Point Sublime on the North Rim.

The entire plant, including roots, may be eaten raw, but it is best when roasted in the hot ashes of a campfire. Many Southwestern Indians ate the plants, and Navajos used it in the treatment of ulcers.

The plants grow 5 to 20 cm (2 to 8 inches) tall. The stems are rather short and are topped by the inflorescence, which may be longer than the stem. Each flowering stalk produces one flower which is tubular with joined petals 15 to 32 mm (5/8 to 1 1/4 inch) long. The free tips of the petals flare outward slightly. The leaves are reduced to tiny scales 5 to 10 mm (1/4 to 3/8 inch) long.

118

Grand Canyon June 1995

MOHAVE ASTER
Xylorhiza tortifolia
Sunflower family
Compositae

119

Perhaps the showiest of Grand Canyon asters, Mohave aster with its large flowers puts forth an unforgettable display in the Inner Canyon after rainy winters. It is found on talus slopes, in dry side canyons, and in other sunny locations from the base of the Redwall Limestone across the Tonto Plateau and down to the Colorado River. Large plants may have 50 flowers in various shades of lavender to pink, all open at once.

Many stems, each 30 to 70 cm (12 to 28 inches) tall, arise from a somewhat woody base. The flowers are 35 to 65 mm (1 3/8 to 2 1/2 inches) in diameter with yellow centers. The lance-shaped leaves, 3 to 6 cm (1 1/4 to 2 3/8 inches) long, are thick and stiff and have large spinose teeth on the edges.

HOARY ASTER

Machaeranthera canescens

Sunflower family

Compositae

120

Hoary aster is the most common of the summer and fall-flowering asters on the South Rim. It is an abundant roadside herb in Grand Canyon Village and along both the East and West Rim Drives from late June until October.

The plant is a biennial or perennial, growing 10 to 40 cm (4 to 16 inches) tall. Numerous violet to purple flowers, each with a yellow center, are 20 to 25 mm (3/4 to 1 inch) across. Hoary aster is very common throughout most of Arizona over a wide elevational range, and is found in western North America from British Columbia south to Arizona and California.

FLEABANE
Erigeron formosissimus
Sunflower family
Compositae

121

This fleabane is a pretty blue or pink-flowered species found only on the North Rim. Flowering from July through September, it grows in deep forests and shady ravines, and has been reported at the North Rim Entrance Station, Cape Royal, Robbers Roost, and Tiyo Ridge.

The plants are perennial with one or more herbaceous stems 10 to 40 cm (4 to 16 inches) tall.

The flowering heads are single or several on a stem with 75 to 150 petals (rays) and a yellow center. The large flowers are about 30 to 40 mm (1 1/4 to 1 1/2 inches) in diameter.

BROWNFOOT PEREZIA
Acourtia wrightii

Sunflower family
Compositae

An evergreen Inner Canyon herb with small, pink, sweet-smelling flowers, perezia may flower much of the year except during cold periods in winter and dry periods in summer. It is often found on shaded slopes and at the base of cliffs, and has been noted at Phantom Ranch, Indian Gardens, Havasu Canyon, and along the Bright Angel Trail.

Indians are reported to have used the root as a styptic.

The plants are perennial with stems usually 60 cm (24 inches) or less tall, often branched at the base or in the inflorescence. The heads contain four to eleven small flowers. The leaves, 6 to 13 cm (2 3/8 to 5 inches) long, are irregularly spiny toothed, fairly thick, and dark green. A tuft of brown wool is seen at the base of the stems; this is a good means of identification when flowers are lacking.

122

PORELEAF
Porophyllum gracile
Sunflower family
Compositae

123

Poreleaf is a small inconspicuous Inner Canyon shrub which usually goes unnoticed until someone steps on it. When crushed, the large glands on the plant release a strong, rather unpleasant odor that is noticeable for a considerable distance. The plants are fairly common in the Inner Gorge, especially on loose, rocky talus slopes and growing from cracks in the Vishnu Schist. Notwithstanding the odor, poreleaf is said to be relished by deer and cattle.

The herbaceous, almost succulent bushes, branched mostly in the lower part, grow 20 to 70 cm (8 to 28 inches) tall, producing rayless flowers which are whitish or purple, streaked with dark purple lines. Small, narrow leaves are present on new growth but they fall off during dry periods. Flowering time is variable, depending on weather, but is usually in March and April and perhaps again in September and October.

Phacelia glechomaefolia

ROCKY MOUNTAIN IRIS
Iris missouriensis
Iris family
Iridaceae

125

Appearing in early summer in the moist meadows of the North Rim, Rocky Mountain iris grows in clumps sometimes forming beautiful displays. Its favored habitats are open areas which are wet in spring, and dry and sunny during June, preceding the summer rains. Ranging in color from pale blue streaked with white to violet blue, the flowers bear a striking resemblance to the larger cultivated iris.

The plant contains a toxic material, irisin, a powerful emetic and cathartic. The rootstalks and leaves are especially poisonous; Plains Indians are reported to have used the toxin as arrowhead poison.

The narrow leaves arise mostly near the base of the plant, and the stem, bearing one or two flowers, is 20 to 50 cm (8 to 20 inches) tall. The rootstalks spread to form clumps which often become quite large in diameter.

VASE-FLOWER, LEATHER-FLOWER
Clematis hirsutissima

Buttercup family
Ranunculaceae

Among the strangest of fruits found in the park is that of the leather flower. Slightly smaller than a baseball, the fuzzy mass consists of numerous seeds each with a tail 4 to 6 cm (1.5 to 2.5 inches) long. The seeds readily separate from the plant and are dispersed as the hairy tails catch hold of the clothing of a person or fur of an animal.

Nearly as distinctive as the fruits are the flowers. The nodding dark purple blossoms resemble an upside-down vase, thus one of the common names.

The sepals (the flower lacks petals) are thick and leathery, from which the name leather flower arises. The flowers are between 2 and 4 cm (1 to 1 1/2 inches) in length and occur singly at the ends of the branches.

Leather flower is found on the North Rim, often in rock outcrops along streamways in dry, open meadows. The flowers appear in June and July, while the fruits may be seen in July and August. The closely related virgin's bower (*Clematis ligusticifolia*) has bunches of smaller white flowers which are open instead of vaselike, and the tails on the seeds are shorter. It is found in canyons on both rims.

BARESTEM LARKSPUR
Delphinium scaposum
Buttercup family
Ranunclaceae

127

Larkspur is a common late spring and early summer wildflower found on both rims and in the pinyon-juniper woodland areas below them. Along the Dripping Springs Trail it is especially abundant in May following wet winters, and its flowering season progresses to June along the North Rim and July in the higher meadows of the North Rim. It is usually found in openings and meadows in the forests, and on open grassy slopes in the Inner Canyon.

Larkspurs contain delphinine and other toxic alkaloids. They may be deadly to cattle, and are apparently less injurious to sheep and horses.

Three species of larkspurs are known to occur in the Grand Canyon. Barestem larkspur flowers vary in color from sky-blue to purplish blue, and adjacent plants often show striking variations in color. The showy part of the flower is

actually the sepals, the upper one elongated backward into a projection called a spur. The less conspicuous petals are lighter in color, the upper two being white.

HILL'S LUPINE

Lupinus hillii

Pea family

Leguminosae

128

Lupines are certainly among the best known and favorite wildflowers in the Southwest. Seven species have been reported from the Grand Canyon, primarily from the rims in spring and summer. Among the most common is Hill's lupine, found flowering mainly from June through August on both rims. Grand Canyon Village, Rowes Well, and Yaki Point are places to see it on the South Rim; on the north side it may be seen along Transept Trail and in many of the sunny, dry meadows. Although some of the species of lupine are difficult to distinguish, they have in common a distinctive leaf of 4 to 8 leaflets arranged palmately; that is, radiating from the same point on the leaf stem. Two of the park's species are low-growing annuals; the rest are rather tall perennial herbs.

Lupines are important nitrogen fixers in otherwise rather sterile pine woodlands and sagebrush desert soils.

Hill's lupine is a perennial with stems usually over 20 cm (8 inches) tall. Its many purple pealike flowers, smaller than those of the other perennial species, are arranged in rather dense elongated clusters. The leaves are silvery-hairy and the leaflets are 2.5 to 5 cm (1 to 2 inches) long. Hill's lupine is found only in central and northern Arizona.

Grand Canyon June 1995

BLUE FLAX
Linum lewisii

Flax family
Linaceae

129

With its sky-blue flowers and tall wandlike stems, flax is a conspicuous plant of many areas in the Grand Canyon region. It is commonly associated with sagebrush in open areas on the South Rim and is also found in pinyon-juniper woodlands. Between Grand Canyon Village and Desert View it is often seen in fields and along roadsides. Look for it before noon, however, as the petals usually drop off by midday, to be replaced by new flowers the next morning. On the North Rim a variant with dark blue petals is found in the dry, high elevation meadows. Flax reaches the Tonto Plateau and is an important element of the spring flora if rainfall is abundant. It flowers in March or April at low elevations and throughout the summer on the rims.

Cultivated flax, an annual Old World species from which flax and linseed oil are obtained, closely resembles the perennial blue flax of the Southwest. Our species was named for Meriwether Lewis of the Lewis and Clark Expedition.

The stems of blue flax grow up to 80 cm (3 feet) tall. They branch at the base forming long, wandlike stems with only short branches above. The handsome flowers have five petals and are 2.5 to 5 cm (1 to 2 inches) across. The leaves are rather small and narrow and are crowded along the stem.

TURPENTINE-BROOM
Thamnosma montana

Rue family
Rutaceae

A rather distinctive plant with its somewhat spinescent, almost leafless stems and large dark blue flowers, turpentine broom is strongly aromatic. Thickly dotted with glands, it has a sharp, citrus-like odor when the stems are crushed or broken. The erect, much-branched shrubs are found in the Inner Canyon from the base of the Redwall Limestone to the Colorado River.

The stems, with a broomlike appearance, grow 10 to 60 cm (4 to 24 inches) tall, becoming spine-tipped. The flowers, with four upright petals, are 8 to 14 mm (3/8 to 5/8 inch) long, and develop a gland-covered fleshy capsule with two spherical lobes. The succulent leaves are small and soon fall off; during most of the year the plant is leafless and photosynthesizes through its green stems.

130

PHACELIA, SCORPIONWEED
Phacelia species
Waterleaf family
Hydrophyllaceae

131

Most of the phacelias are spring annuals, and they vary tremendously in their abundance according to the amount of winter rain. Of the 18 species known to occur in the park, five are pictured here. All occur in the Inner Canyon, mostly on the Tonto Plateau and in the Inner Gorge. The second common name is derived from the coiling of the inflorescence in some species, resembling a scorpion's tail.

The Arizona phacelias fall into two groups, one with round, toothed leaves and the other with longer, deeply divided leaves. *Phacelia crenulata,* in the latter group, is the most widely distributed species in the state and is a common spring annual in the Inner Gorge, often seen on sand dunes or in gravelly washes. It is covered with glandular hairs to which some people have an allergic reaction.

Phacelia pedicellata is also very glandular and may cause dermatitis. It has lighter-colored flowers and several dense, coiled inflorescences at the top of the plant. It is found in the Inner Gorge, often in the schist.

The three round-leaved species are delicate annuals, common in wet years and virtually unseen when there is insufficient rain. *Phacelia glechomaefolia* is the largest and, with its lavender or purple flowers, a very handsome plant.

P. crenulata

P. pedicellata

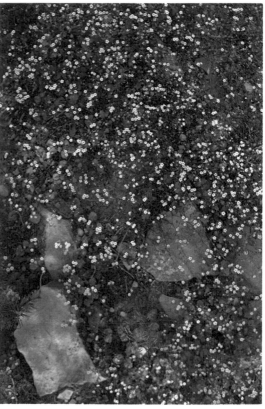

P. filiformis

It is most often seen in the Inner Gorge in the western part of the Grand Canyon, often making spectacular springtime displays in remote areas where few people see them.

Phacelia filiformis is a somewhat smaller plant, with delicate, lighter-colored flowers. It reaches as high as the rims and may be seen in April along the Clear Creek Trail and in May along the Dripping Springs Trail.

Phacelia rotundifolia has tiny white flowers and dark green succulent leaves with purplish or brownish sticky-glandular stems. It is an Inner Gorge species usually found in places where the plants receive little sun, such as under rock overhangs or in narrow side canyons. The Tapeats Sandstone provides many protected spots where this plant is often found. A good place to see it is along the Clear Creek Trail where it passes through the Tapeats.

The phacelias in the Grand Canyon are not particularly common, and the individual species do not even have recognized common names. They are beautiful little plants, however, and if one is fortunate to be in the Canyon when they happen to be flowering they are well worth a close look.

132

P. glechomaefolia

P. rotundifolia

DESERT SAGE, PURPLE SAGE
Salvia dorrii
Mint family
Labiatae

133

A small, intricately-branched shrub of the Inner Canyon, desert sage is a handsome plant with its blue and purple flowers. The flowers are actually blue, with several maroon or purple bracts under each cluster, giving a rich purple hue to the shrub when seen from a distance. Flowering in April and May, the plants are fairly common, especially in dry washes and along several of the trails between the Supai Formation and the Tonto Plateau. The photograph was taken in a small arroyo on the Plateau Point Trail a short distance from Indian Gardens.

Desert sage is a common shrub in the Great Basin and is near its southern limit in the Grand Canyon. The garden herb sage is from a cultivated European member of the genus. Sagebrush, the dominant shrub in most of the Great Basin Desert, is a member of the Sunflower family and is unrelated.

Desert sage is a low compact shrub 10 to 50 cm (4 to 20 inches) tall with rigid, often spinescent branches. The flowers are in a series of dense inflorescences toward the ends of the branches. The many small narrow to rounded leaves are silvery-green in color.

TOADFLAX PENSTEMON; BEARDTONGUE

Penstemon linarioides

SOUTH RIM
NORTH RIM
Flowers: June-September

Figwort family
Scrophulariaceae

Although the flowers of toadflax penstemon give away its identity, the shrubby growth habit of the plant is very different from the other penstemons. With numerous short, woody stems and narrow needle-like leaves, the mat-like plants lack the broad basal leaves and tall flowering stalks of other penstemons.

Toadflax penstemon is a common summer-flowering plant in the woodlands and forests of both rims. Its attractive purple flowers may be seen from June into August around Grand Canyon Village and along the East Rim Drive on the South Rim and at Tiyo Point on the North Rim.

The plants have a branching root system putting out erect stems 5 to 35 cm (2 to 14 inches) long with a few flowers toward the end of the branches. The flowers are about 14 to 17 mm (5/8 to 3/4 inch) long and inflated to an almost globose shape in contrast to the tubular flowers of the red penstemons. Four of the five stamens are fertile and produce pollen. The common name beardtongue is derived from the fifth stamen which has a dense beard of fine yellow hairs. The leaves are very narrow and are about 5 to 25 mm (1/4 to 1 inch) long, often more crowded toward the base of the stem.

Grand Canyon June 1995

THICKLEAF PENSTEMON
Penstemon pachyphyllus

Figwort family
Scrophulariaceae

135

The common purple penstemon of the South Rim, thickleaf penstemon is abundant in the Grand Canyon Village area and may be seen flowering from April to June along the South Rim Trail between the Visitor Center and Yavapai Point. The bluish-purple flowers are arranged in clusters at short intervals along the stem. Its common name is derived from the thickish, almost succulent, bluish-green leaves. While near its southern limit at Grand Canyon, the thickleaf penstemon is a common species in Utah and Nevada.

The plants often put forth several flowering stems 25 to 65 cm (10 to 26 inches) tall. The flowers have a short tube, which is inflated but not as strongly as that of toadflax penstemon (*Penstemon linarioides*). Five lobes of the joined petals, two above and three below, provide a "landing platform" for bumblebees, the main pollinators.

Grand Canyon June 1995

WATER SPEEDWELL
Veronica anagallis-aquatica
Figwort family
Scrophulariaceae

Of the four species of speedwell found in the park, this is the only one which combines a strictly aquatic habit and sessile leaves placed directly on the stem. It is the most common species in the Inner Canyon, where it is found along the shores of the Colorado River and in various flowing sidestreams. Along the Bright Angel Trail it grows in Garden Creek below Indian Gardens, where this photograph was taken.

The perennial, leafy-stemmed plants grow 20 to 90 cm (8 to 36 inches) tall with clusters of tiny blue to bluish-lilac flowers arising from the leaf axils. Each of the round, slightly asymmetric flowers is 4 to 5 mm (1/4 inch) across with tiny darker rays going from the center of the flower to the outside. Although they may go unnoticed from a distance, the delicate beauty of these flowers is certainly worth a close look.

PARRY BELLFLOWER
Campanula parryi
Bellflower family
Campanulaceae

137

Parry bellflower is an attractive purple or blue-flowered plant found most often in sunny mountain meadows on the North Rim. Flowering anytime from July into September, the slender, narrow-leaved perennial usually has only one flower which almost appears disproportionately large atop the delicate plant.

The erect stems of Parry bellflower grow 6 to 30 cm (2 1/2 to 12 inches) tall, and the bell-shaped flower with its five fused petals is about 10 to 25 mm (3/8 to 1 inch) long. Its basal leaves are narrowly oblong, 2 to 6 cm (3/4 to 2 1/2 inches) long; the stem leaves are neither as wide nor as long. The colorful plants grace subalpine meadows from Wyoming south to northern Arizona and New Mexico.

BIBLIOGRAPHY

Benson, Lyman. 1969. *The Cacti of Arizona*. Third Edition. Tucson: The University of Arizona Press.

Buchanan, Hayle. 1974. *Living Color: Wildflower Communities of Bryce Canyon and Cedar Breaks*. Bryce Canyon, Utah: Bryce Canyon Natural History Association.

Elmore, F.H., and J.R. Janish. 1976. *Shrubs and Trees of the Southwest Uplands*. Globe, Arizona: Southwest Parks and Monuments Association.

Kearney, T.H., and R.H. Peebles, and Collaborators. 1960. *Arizona Flora*, with supplement by J.T. Howell and Elizabeth McClintock, and Collaborators. Berkeley: University of California Press.

Kirk, Donald R. 1970. *Wild Edible Plants of the Western United States*. Healdsburg, California: Naturegraph Publishers

McDougall, Walter B. 1973. *Seed Plants of Northern Arizona*. Flagstaff: Museum of Northern Arizona Press.

Nelson, Ruth A. 1976. *Plants of Zion National Park*. Springdale, Utah: Zion Natural History Association.

Niehaus, Theodore F., Charles R. Ripper, and Virginia Savage. 1984. *A Field Guide to Southwestern and Texas Wildflowers*. Peterson Field Guide Series No. 31. Houghton Mifflin Co.

Phillips, Arthur M., III. 1977. "Grand Canyon Biology: A Botanist's View." Plateau 49(4): 11-17.

Phillips, Arthur M., III, and Barbara G. Phillips. 1984. Spring Wildflowers of Northern Arizona. Plateau 55(3). Museum of Northern Arizona.

Phillips, Arthur M., III, and Barbara G. Phillips. 1987. High Country Wildflowers. Plateau 58(3). Museum of Northern Arizona.

Phillips, Barbara G., Arthur M. Phillips, III, and Marilyn Ann Schmidt Bernzott. 1987. Annotated Checklist of Vascular Plants of Grand Canyon National Park. Grand Canyon Natural History Association Monograph No. 7. Grand Canyon, AZ.

Taylor, R.J., and R.W. Valum. 1974. *Wildflowers 2: Sagebrush Country*. Beaverton, Oregon: The Touchstone Press.

Whiting, Alfred F. 1950. *Ethnobotany of the Hopi*. Museum of Northern Arizona Bulletin 15. Flagstaff: Northern Arizona Society of Science and Art.

GLOSSARY

Annual—a plant which germinates from seed, flowers, sets seed, and dies within a single growing season.

Apex—the point or tip of a leaf, flowering stalk, or stem.

Areoles—the points on the fleshy stem of a cactus at which the spines arise.

Axil—the upper angle at the point where a leaf is joined to a stem.

Basal—arising or growing from the base of the stem, at or near ground level.

Biennial—a plant that lives two years, producing leaves the first year and flowering and dying the second year.

Bract—a modified leaf often associated with a flower, sometimes brightly colored and resembling the petals.

Compound leaf—a divided leaf, with two or more separate parts called leaflets.

Glochids—tiny needle-like spines that occur in the areoles of cholla and prickly pear cacti. Appearing like hairs, they are easily and painfully detached.

Inflorescence—the flower cluster of a plant.

Lobes—indentations in the margin of a leaf.

Nodes—points on a stem where leaves or side branches are attached.

Obovate leaf—egg-shaped, with the narrow end at the base.

Palmate—applied to a compound leaf whose divisions are arranged like the outspread fingers of a hand.

Perennial—a plant which lives more than two years.

Perfoliate—upper leaves which join around the stem at their bases, giving the appearance of the stem passing through the center of a disk.

Petiole—the stalk of a leaf, found between the blade and the stem of the plant.

Plumose—plume-like or feather-like.

Prehensile—applied to specialized structures (tendrils) of vine-like plants which allow the plants to climb by twisting around other vegetation or objects.

Prostrate stems—growing along the ground, without upright branches.

Rays—in most members of the Sunflower Family, the parts of the flower that appear like petals. Actually each ray is a strap-like extension of a single tiny flower; the "flowers" of members of this family are composed of many small individual flowers.

Receptacle—disk-shaped structure at the base of a flower to which the flower parts are attached.

Root crown—the top of a root; juncture between the root and the stem.

Rootstock—a horizontal, often enlarged, underground stem, producing upright leafy shoots on the upper side and roots on the lower side.

Rosette—a circular cluster of leaves at the base of a plant.

Sepals—the usually green outermost segments of the flower, immediately outside the petals.

Sessile—attached directly by the base, without a stalk, as a leaf without a petiole.

Spinescent—more or less spiny; spinelike.

Stamen—the structure of a flower which produces the pollen.

Stolon—a horizontal stem at or below the surface of the ground that gives rise to a new plant at its tip.

Style—structure at the top of the ovary in the flower, containing the pollen-receptive part at the tip and sometimes elongating in fruit.

Taproot—a stout, vertical root often with stored food, like a carrot.

Tendril—specialized grasping structure arising at the tip of a leaf or on a stem, in vine-like plants used for climbing (see prehensile).

Tube—in a flower whose petals are connected, the elongated part below the outer tip of the flower.